In Our Hands

In Our Hands

A Plan to Replace the Welfare State

Charles Murray

REVISED AND UPDATED EDITION

THE AEI PRESS

Publisher for the American Enterprise Institute
WASHINGTON, DC

Distributed to the Trade by National Book Network, 15200 NBN Way, Blue Ridge Summit, PA 17214. To order call toll free 1-800-462-6420 or 1-717-794-3800. For all other inquiries please contact the AEI Press, 1789 Massachusetts Ave., NW, Washington, DC 20036 or call 1-800-862-5801.

ISBN-13: 978-1-4422-6071-9 (paperback)
ISBN-10: 1-4422-6071-8 (paperback)
ISBN-13: 978-1-4422-6072-6 (ebook)
ISBN-10: 1-4422-6072-6 (ebook)

Printed in the United States of America

Contents

List of Illustrations

Ground Rules

An old joke has three men stuck at the bottom of a hole, each presenting his plan to escape. I have forgotten who the first two are, but the third is an economist. When his turn comes he begins by saying, "First, we assume a ladder."

This book puts me in the position of the economist. The ladder I will be describing to you would work if it existed, but today's American politicians will not build it. I must ask you to suspend disbelief and play along.

My part of the bargain is to be realistic about everything else, presenting evidence that the policy is financially feasible and would produce the desirable results I claim—not in a utopia, but in the United States of the twenty-first century.

Preface to the 2016 Edition

The original version of *In Our Hands* published in 2006 predicted that the costs of the existing system and my plan for a universal basic income would cross in 2011. I was two years off, thanks to the Great Recession and the stimulus spending that followed. By 2015, the crossover point had been passed for six years. Discarding the welfare state in favor of a universal basic income is no longer something that would be economically feasible in America's future. It is economically feasible right now.

Three other considerations prompted me to restate *In Our Hands'* case. First, the rising costs of entitlement programs require that something be done—not in the distant future, but within the next few administrations—to prevent a fiscal crisis. This reality makes my solution more politically feasible now than it was a decade ago. Second, the increasing breakdown of the American working class that I described a few years ago in *Coming Apart* adds new urgency to changes in policy that would resuscitate America's civic culture. I believe a universal basic income has unique potential for doing so. The third reason was on the distant horizon when I wrote *In Our Hands* but is now looming: Advances in technology are not just automating millions of manual jobs, but will soon be displacing millions of white-collar workers.[1] In the decades ahead, a life well-lived will often have to be one that does not involve a job traditionally defined. A universal basic income will be an essential part of the transition to a world unlike any in the history of our species.

Initially, I intended to do no more than replace the old numbers with new ones. But doing so wasn't possible. Since 2006, the way that the federal government reports budget figures has changed, trend lines for budget projections have changed, and inflation required me to increase the size of the guaranteed grant. The arithmetic for *In Our Hands* had to be redone from scratch.

The text of *In Our Hands* also changed far more than I anticipated. Apparently there is no such thing as prose a decade old that I don't want to fiddle with. Most obviously, I have discarded "The Plan" as the label for my solution—a label I was never happy with—and replaced it with "UBI," standing for "universal basic income." In some cases, intervening events required changes in the presentation—the Affordable Care Act's effect on the chapter on health care is an example. Other changes are cosmetic ones intended to make the text more accessible or engaging. In a few instances, I hope that 10 years of mulling over these issues enabled me to elaborate or tighten an argument. But my guiding principles in 2006 remain unchanged, and so does *In Our Hands*' message.

Charles Murray
Burkittsville, Maryland
March 19, 2016

Introduction

A Short Statement of the Argument

America is wealthy beyond the imagining of earlier generations. Every year, the American government redistributes more than $2 trillion of that wealth to provide for retirement, health care, and the alleviation of poverty. We still have millions of people without comfortable retirements, without adequate health care, and living in poverty. Only a government can spend so much money so ineffectually. The solution is to give the money to the people.

A Longer Statement of the Argument

The European and American welfare states evolved under the twin assumptions that resources were scarce and that government could allocate them effectively.

The first assumption was true during the first half of the twentieth century, in this sense: No country had ever been so rich that its wealth, divided evenly among everyone, would provide everyone with a comfortable living. After World War II, in a few countries, wealth increased so much that there *was* enough money to go around—a landmark event in human history. It was technically possible for no one to be poor. Much of the energy behind the social turmoil of the 1960s was fueled by this revolutionary change.

Enter the second of the assumptions, that governments could allocate resources effectively. During the early decades of the welfare state, it seemed simple. The indigent elderly depend on charity, so let the government provide everyone with a guaranteed pension. The unemployed husband and father cannot find a job, so let the government give him useful work to do and pay him for it. Some people who are sick cannot afford to go to a private physician, so let the government pay for health care.

It turned out not to be simple after all. The act of giving pensions increased the probability that people reached old age needing them. Governments had a hard time finding useful work for unemployed people and were ineffectual employers even when they did. The demand for medical care outstripped the supply. But, despite the complications, these were the easy tasks. Scandinavia and the Netherlands—small, ethnically homogeneous societies, with traditions of work, thrift, neighborliness, and social consensus—did them best.

Traditions decay when the reality facing the new generation changes. The habit of thrift decays if there is no penalty for not saving. The work ethic decays if there is no penalty for not working. Neighborliness decays when neighbors are no longer needed. Social consensus decays with immigration. Even the easy tasks became hard as time went on.

During the second half of the twentieth century, the welfare state confronted accelerating increases in the number of people who were not just poor, but who behaved in destructive ways that ensured they would remain poor, sometimes living off their fellow citizens, sometimes preying on them. As their numbers grew, they acquired a new name: the underclass. The underclass grew first in the nation that was the largest and ethnically most heterogeneous: the United States. As the years passed, poor young men increasingly reached adulthood unprepared to work even when jobs were available. They were more disposed to commit crimes. Poor young women more often bore children without a husband. Poor children more often were born to parents who were incompetent to nurture them. When it came to solving these problems, it was obvious by the 1980s that government had failed. Then the evidence grew that government had exacerbated the problems it was trying to solve. As the Americans were making these discoveries, an underclass also began to emerge in the European welfare states.

That the easy tasks of the welfare state became hard and that underclasses are growing throughout the Western world are neither coincidences nor inevitable byproducts of modernity. The welfare state produces its own destruction. The process takes decades to play out, but it is inexorable. First, the welfare state degrades the traditions of work, thrift, and neighborliness that enabled a society to work at the outset; then it spawns social and economic problems that it is powerless to solve. The welfare state as we have come to know it is everywhere within decades of financial and social bankruptcy.

The libertarian solution is to prevent the government from redistributing money in the first place. Imagine for a moment that the $2 trillion that the US government spends on transfer payments were left instead in the hands of the people who started with it. If I could wave a magic wand, that would be my solution. It is a case I have made elsewhere.[2] Leave the wealth where it originates, and watch how its many uses, individual and collaborative, enable civil society to meet the needs that government cannot.

But that is a solution that upward of 90 percent of the population will dismiss. Some will dismiss it because they do not accept that people will behave in the cooperative and compassionate ways that I believe they would. But there is another sticking point for many people with which I am sympathetic: People are unequal in the abilities that lead to economic success in life.

To the extent that inequality of wealth is grounded in the way people freely choose to conduct their lives, I do not find it troubling. People are complicated bundles of skills and motivations, strengths and weaknesses, and so are their roads to happiness. Some people pursue happiness in ways that tend to be accompanied by large incomes, others in ways that tend to be accompanied by lower incomes. In a free society, these choices are made voluntarily, with psychic rewards balanced against monetary rewards. Income inequality is accordingly large. So what?

Inequality of wealth grounded in unequal abilities is different. For most of us, the luck of the draw cuts several ways: one person is not handsome, but is smart; another is not as smart, but is industrious; and still another is not as industrious, but is charming. This kind of inequality of human capital is enriching, making life more interesting for everyone. But some portion of the population gets the short end of the stick on several dimensions. As the number of dimensions grows, so does the punishment for being unlucky. When a society tries to redistribute the goods of life to compensate the most unlucky, its heart is in the right place, however badly the thing has worked out in practice.

Hence this book. The argument starts by accepting that the American government will continue to spend a huge amount of money on income transfers. It then contends that we should take all of that money and give it back to the American people in cash grants. The chapters that follow explain how it might be done, why it is economically feasible, and the good that would follow.

PART I

Framework

1

The Plan

A year after the end of World War II, an economist from the University of Chicago named George Stigler wrote an article criticizing the minimum wage as a way of combating poverty. In passing, he mentioned an idea that had been suggested to him by a young colleague, Milton Friedman: Instead of raising the minimum wage or trying to administer complicated welfare systems, just give poor people the cash difference between what they make and the income necessary for a decent standard of living. The idea came to be called a negative income tax, or NIT.[3]

In the early 1960s, Friedman formally proposed the NIT as a replacement for all income transfers.[4] A few years later Robert Lampman, a scholar of the left, also endorsed it, and a political constituency for experimenting with the NIT began to grow.[5] During the 1970s, the federal government sponsored test versions of the NIT in selected sites in Iowa, New Jersey, Indiana, Pennsylvania, and, most ambitiously, in Denver and Seattle.

The experimental NIT produced disappointing results. The work disincentives were substantial and ominously largest among the youngest recipients. Marital breakup was higher among participants than among the control group in most of the sites.[6] No headlines announced these results, but the NIT quietly disappeared from the policy debate.

The experimental NIT was nothing like Friedman's idea—it augmented the existing transfer payments instead of replacing them. But the experimental NIT did convincingly demonstrate that a simple floor on income is a bad idea. There is no incentive to work at jobs that pay less than the floor, and the marginal tax rates on jobs that pay a little more than the floor are punishingly high. But as the amount of money that the United States spends on the poor continued to increase during the next four decades while the official poverty remained effectively unchanged,[7] the underlying appeal of the NIT persisted: If we're spending that much money to eradicate poverty, why not just give poor people enough cash so that they won't be poor, and be done with it?

Friedman's concept was valid. The devil was in the details. A variant of the NIT puts it within our power to end poverty, provide for comfortable retirement and medical care for everyone, and—as a bonus that is probably more important than any of the immediate effects—revitalize American civil society.

The variant is a universal basic income—UBI for short.[8] I propose a plan to implement a UBI that converts all transfer payments to a single cash payment for everyone age 21 and older. It would require a constitutional amendment that I am not competent to frame in legal language, but its sense is easy to express:

> Henceforth, federal, state, and local governments shall make no law nor establish any program that transfers general tax revenues to some citizens and not to others, whether those transfers consist of money or in-kind benefits. All programs currently providing such benefits are to be terminated. The funds formerly allocated to them are to be used instead to provide every citizen with a Universal Basic Income beginning at age twenty-one and continuing until death. The maximum annual value of the grant at the program's outset is to be $13,000, of which $3,000 must be devoted to catastrophic health insurance.

The UBI does not require much in the way of bureaucratic apparatus. Its administration consists of computerized electronic deposits to bank accounts, plus resources to identify fraud. Here are the nuts and bolts:

- *Universal passport.* At the time of the UBI's adoption, each US citizen receives a passport that has the same official status and uses as the current passport. Subsequently, a passport is issued to each US citizen at birth.[9] This passport also establishes eligibility for the UBI.

- *A known bank account.* A condition of receiving the grant is that the citizen notify the government of an account at a US financial institution with an American Bankers Association routing number. The grant is electronically deposited into the account monthly.[10] No bank account, no grant.

One Step at a Time

Describing the UBI in the language of a constitutional amendment raises a host of practical questions. For example, how would local and state expenditures on transfer programs be captured to fund the UBI? It would be an important question if we were about to have a congressional debate on an actual constitutional amendment. But we are stellar distances away from that point. In this instance, the limited proposition I defend is that we are spending so much money on transfers that the UBI is affordable and emphatically preferable to the current system. Let's begin by thinking about whether that proposition is true.

The same distinction will recur throughout the book, as I focus on the question "Is this doable if we want it badly enough?" while ignoring problems that would need to be worked out if we got to the point of debating the UBI in Congress. Unless people who care about social policy are willing to do this, the solutions we can consider will always amount to tinkering.

- *Reimbursement schedule.* Personal income has no effect on the grant until that income reaches $30,000. From $30,000 to $60,000, a surtax is levied that reimburses the grant up to a maximum of half its total. The surtax is 10 percent of incremental earned income for first $5,000 after $30,000. The surtax increases by 4 percentage points with each subsequent $5,000, maxing out at 30 percent for the $5,000 from $55,000 to $59,999. Persons making $60,000 or more get a UBI of $6,500.

- *Catastrophic health insurance.* The sole stipulation about how the $13,000 is to be used is that $3,000 be devoted to a catastrophic health insurance policy. The reasons for this are explained in Chapter 3.

- *Eligibility.* The definition of personal income is based on individuals regardless of marital status or living arrangements. Thus, a wife whose income from her own sources, whether job earnings, dividends, or

Transfers Are Not Public Goods

The benefits that a government provides to the governed span a range from public goods classically defined at one extreme to pure transfers at the other.

Public goods classically defined are ones that are available to everyone on equal terms, and that can be consumed by one citizen without making the good less available to another. The best examples are national defense, police protection, and, in more recent times, clean air.

Benefits that are bestowed only on some citizens, groups, or organizations can be defended as public goods in a loose sense ("It is good for a society as a whole if the homeless are given shelter" or "It is good for a society as a whole if the family farm is protected"), but they are qualitatively different from classic public goods. The immediate benefit (shelter for the homeless or an agricultural subsidy) goes to certain identifiable individuals and not to others. Furthermore, two citizens cannot jointly share the good as they can jointly share national defense or clean air. The bed one person occupies in a homeless shelter means one less bed available for everyone else. When a farmer gets his subsidy check, that money cannot be used for any other citizen. Following common usage, I label these benefits *transfers*. Tax dollars are taken from some citizens and given to others in cash, kind, or services. Whether the transfers are justified is not at issue at the moment, merely the fact that they are transfers.

interest, is less than $30,000 will get the full $13,000 no matter how much her husband makes.

- *Changes in the size of the grant.* As time goes on, even low inflation will erode the purchasing power of the grant. One option is to link its size to median personal earned income.[11] Another is for Congress to make ad hoc adjustments to it. A third is to link the UBI to inflation. I leave the provision for adjusting the size of the grant open. The government's projections of the costs and benefits of maintaining the current system customarily assume zero inflation, and so will my projections of the costs and benefits of the UBI.

- *Tax revenues.* The calculations assume that the tax system continues to generate revenue at the current rate without specifying how the tax code might be changed. Whether current Social Security and Medicare taxes should remain as they are, or whether the amounts of money they generate should be folded into individual or corporate taxes, are separate issues that I do not try to address.

- *The programs to be eliminated.* The UBI eliminates programs that are unambiguously transfers: Social Security, Medicare, Medicaid, welfare programs, social service programs, agricultural subsidies, and corporate welfare. It does not apply a strict libertarian definition of transfer, leaving activities such as state-funded education, funding for transportation infrastructure, and the postal service in place. A list of the programs that the UBI replaces is given in Appendix A.

That's the UBI. A cash grant, with a surtax, funded by eliminating the transfers that currently exist. I require that $3,000 be devoted to health care, but otherwise I will argue that many of the best effects of the UBI are fostered by the least direction: "Here's the money. Use it as you see fit. Your life is in your hands."

2

Basic Finances

A universal basic income of $13,000 a year for every adult American system is not only within our reach. It is cheaper than the system we have in place and will become much cheaper in the years to come.

The crossover year in which the UBI became cheaper than the existing system was 2009. Figure 2-1 shows the actual costs of the current system and of the UBI (if it had been implemented) through 2014 and the projected costs of the alternatives through 2020.

Figure 2-1. Costs of the UBI and the Current System, 2000–2020

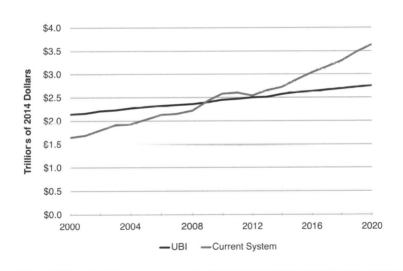

Sources: See Appendix B.

As of 2014, the UBI would have been $212 billion less than the current system. By 2020, it is projected to be $931 billion cheaper than the current system. Here's the arithmetic that produced the graph:

Nota Bene

Every dollar amount in this book, in the text or in charts, is expressed in 2014 dollars.

Cost of the UBI as of 2014

Eligible Population. In 2014, the resident population of the United States age 21 and older was about 232 million persons. Immigrants over 21 (legal or illegal) who are not citizens and incarcerated criminals over 21, totaling roughly 20 million of the 232 million, would not be eligible for the grant.[12] I do not correct the projected costs of the UBI for them. This is an example of a principle I tried to apply generally: When projecting the costs of the UBI, err on the high side; when calculating and projecting the costs of the current system, err on the low side. The result is that my conclusions about the financial feasibility of the UBI have a cushion.

Reimbursement. As described in Chapter 1, my plan for the UBI includes a partial clawback of the grant through a surtax beginning at $30,000 of personal income. Appendix B walks through the calculation of how many people in 2014 would have gotten the full $13,000, how many would have gotten $6,500, and how many were at the incremental income steps between $30,000 and $60,000. As of 2014, the UBI could have been implemented for the 232 million Americans age 21 and older for $2.58 trillion.

Expenditures on Programs That the UBI Replaces. Appendix A lists the programs to be eliminated. By far the biggest are Social Security, Medicare, and Medicaid. In all, the programs to be eliminated spent $2.77 trillion in 2014. Those costs are taken from the historical tables for the federal budget published by the Office of Management and Budget (hereafter OMB-HB) and the census of governments conducted by the Census Bureau.

Projections of Future Costs

Each line item in the OMB-HB tables used to calculate the actual costs from 2000–2014 also includes projections through 2020, drawing on the OMB's own analyses and those of the Congressional Budget Office. The projection of the costs of the UBI uses census projections for population by sex and age, applied to the income distribution by sex and age as of 2014.

How much confidence can we have in these projections of costs? To give a sense of the answer for the projected costs of the current system, the next figure shows actual outlays for by far the biggest cost component of the current system, federal transfers to individuals, from 1980 through 2014.

Figure 2-2. The Persistence of the Underlying Trend in Transfers to Individuals

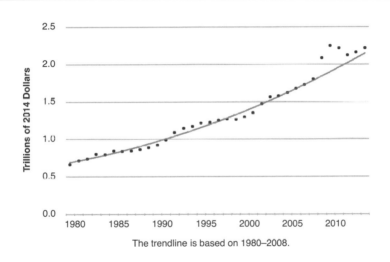

The trendline is based on 1980–2008.

Source: OMB-HB.

The federal government's response to the financial meltdown of 2008 caused a visible spike in government spending in the subsequent three years, but it didn't do much to the underlying trend line. Look at the gray line. It was calculated based on data from 1980–2008, ending just before the spike in 2009. As you can see, expenditures by 2012–2014 were only slightly above what would have been predicted on the basis of 1980–2008. The reason for this is the huge role of Social Security, Medicare, and Medicaid. Their costs are driven by demographics, not economic events.[13]

Now I turn to the projection of the cost of UBI, which assumes that the income distribution as of 2014 can be applied to the next several years. Changes in the job market can obviously affect that assumption. Insofar as wages increase, the per capita cost of the UBI will diminish. Insofar as labor force participation decreases or unemployment increases, the per capita cost of the UBI will increase.

But the cost of of the UBI is less sensitive to such changes than you might expect. Consider the projection of costs of the UBI in the original edition of *In Our Hands*. In 2002, the year used as the baseline for the calculations, the labor force participation (LFP) rate was 66.6 percent, the unemployment rate was 5.8 percent, and median personal income in 2014 dollars for people 21 and older was $28,952.[14] In 2014, the LFP rate was lower, 62.9 percent; the unemployment rate was higher, 6.2 percent; and median personal income was lower, $26,000. It would seem that projections of the UBI in 2014 based on the income distribution in 2002 would significantly underestimate the cost of the UBI in 2014. In fact, the projected cost of the UBI for 2014 using the 2002 income distribution was $2.56 trillion compared with the $2.58 trillion estimate for 2014 using the 2014 income distribution—a difference of less than 1 percentage point.[15]

The reality is that even large changes in the economy don't shift the income distribution enough to make much difference in the affordability of the UBI. During the Great Recession, unemployment jumped from 5.8 percent in 2008 to 9.3 percent in 2009. The cost of the UBI if it had been implemented in 2009 was $43 billion larger than it had been in 2008, whereas the increase from 2007 to 2008 was just $22 billion. But the difference between $43 billion and $22 billion amounted to less than 1 percent of the UBI's 2008 cost—which is why the trend line for the UBI shown in Figure 2-1, which opened the chapter, shows only the slightest bump from 2008 to 2009, compared with the spike in spending for the costs of the current system.

This overview of finances leaves loose ends. Appendixes A and B elaborate on details that I have skipped here; Chapter 7 takes up the question of work disincentives and presents the reasons for thinking they would be acceptable. But it is important to begin with the basics of the arithmetic:

- The amount that this nation already spends and is committed to spending on transfers is huge and rising fast.

- Divide these huge, rising amounts by the number of people over 21, and a $13,000 per-year grant is already cheaper than the current system. By 2020, it can be expected to cost close to $1 trillion less per year than the current system.

- This comparison between the UBI and the current system holds true even when unrealistically conservative assumptions are made in calculating the present and future costs of the UBI.

Holding those thoughts in mind, it is time to consider what the UBI would accomplish.

PART II

Immediate Effects

3

Health Care

The next five chapters explore the immediate effects of the UBI on health care, retirement, poverty, the underclass, and work disincentives. I begin with health care because health care is *sui generis* in two respects. It directly affects matters of life and death and is also the most perversely structured and operated sector of the American economy. One option would be to implement the UBI independently of health care. But a rational and affordable health care system is so easily within our reach that it could and should be part of the UBI, so I present the case. By *easily* I don't mean politically easy. Achieving a rational and affordable health care system is politically impossible as of 2016. But it is technically easy.

The rest of the chapter may be read as an elaboration on this analogy: *Taking care of your health care needs should be like keeping your car on the road.* We pay for gas, oil, and routine maintenance with cash or a credit card, the same way we deal with other costs of daily life. We have auto insurance to protect us in the event of a major crash and to cover our liability. Not only that, we are required to have insurance covering our liability. We are not legally permitted to take our car on the road without it.

These costs usually add up to at least a few thousands dollars a year, but people deal with them. Even without a single government program to subsidize cars for poor people, almost three out of four people below the official poverty line own a vehicle.[16] The same principles can make health insurance work in the presence of the UBI. The UBI requires the equivalent of legally mandatory auto insurance, using part of the grant—I have specified $3,000—to purchase catastrophic health insurance, and leaves the rest up to us. Doing so affordably—meaning that the compulsory insurance package eats up a reasonable portion of the UBI—is possible given a few reforms.

First some background, after which I will describe three specific and essential reforms.

The Context for Reform

The Inevitability of Choices. Until well into the twentieth century, the things that medicine could do to extend life and improve quality of life were limited to a few surgical operations and inoculations plus medications that mainly alleviated symptoms. The commercial production of antibiotics was one landmark change in this situation. Another was a rapid expansion in surgical capabilities. But these developments didn't gain momentum until the 1930s. It has been only about 80 years since the quality of health care began to make much difference to large numbers of people. Now health care can prolong life and improve its quality in myriad ways. Everybody understandably wants everything that contemporary medicine has to offer. Politicians around the world compete to promise voters that they will get it, provided by the government, and people around the world tend to vote for them.

Politicians cannot admit the brutal truth: No government can make good on the promise of universal state-of-the-art health care, not even in a country as rich as the United States. Medical advances have produced too many possibilities to give everyone everything. In even the richest nations, choices need to be made about who gets what care, based on the same question that underlies every purchase: "Is it worth it?" The issue is who makes that choice—an individual who needs the care, or a government that doles it out.

The Falling Real Costs of Health Care. The health care story has a bright side, however, if only we would stop to think about it: Except at its frontier, health care should be getting cheaper. The real costs of the routine things that keep you healthy and cure you of many ailments have been going down. *Real costs* means the actual dollar costs of medical equipment, pharmaceuticals, facilities, and labor for accomplishing a given medical outcome.

The biggest reduction in costs has been produced by antibiotics, which have converted many formerly painful, expensive, and mortal ailments into minor problems. But the reduction in real costs has occurred in many things physicians do. Wounds that used to require stitching often can be closed with adhesives. Blood tests that used to require labor-intensive analysis are now done automatically by machines. Ulcers that used to require surgery are now controlled through inexpensive pills.

Cost per outcome has been dropping for many of the high-tech medical technologies. Laparoscopic surgery is an example: The cost of laparoscopic equipment is greater than the cost of a scalpel and retractors for traditional surgery, but the patient goes home sooner, saving hospitalization costs. Those savings occur with every operation, while the cost of the laparoscopic equipment is amortized over hundreds of operations.

Even the labor costs of health care should be falling. The potential reductions in labor costs are limited because health care will always be more labor-intensive than most industries, but productivity per employee is rising nonetheless. Remote monitoring of symptoms means that fewer nurses can keep track of more patients. Improvements in technologies for everything from hospital beds to food preparation increase the productivity of support staff. If other forces weren't getting in the way, the cost of keeping a person in a hospital bed for a day would be going down.

The one way in which the real cost of health care naturally increases is through the expansion of the outcomes that medicine can achieve. They account for only a small proportion of the advances in medical science. The rest of the improvements involve better or more certain ways of achieving existing outcomes, and those are the ones for which costs should usually be stable or falling.

The Consequences of Shielding People from Choosing. The rising costs of routine health care are owed to the ways in which the laws governing health care ensure that costs rise. They are all variations on the same theme: Most Americans have employer health insurance, Medicare, or Medicaid, all of which have one thing in common: They usually shield the ultimate consumers of health care—you and me—from making the choice "Is it worth it?" Three examples will illustrate.

Example #1: Routine medical problems. You trip on the basement stairs and end up with a two-inch gash in your arm that needs stitches and a tetanus booster. Now, you go to your private physician or the emergency room. The bill will reach three figures, perhaps four if you go to the ER, paid by your employer-provided insurance. If you have no coverage and no cash, the cost of your visit to the ER will be passed on to the hospital's other patients—which is to say, passed on to insurance companies. If you are poor and on

Medicaid, the cost will be passed on to government—which is to say, passed on to taxpayers.

Suppose the money were coming out of your own pocket. In that case, it might occur to you that you don't need to see a physician. What you need is a medical technician in a walk-in clinic that sells treatment for minor medical problems. The wholesale cost of the antiseptics, gauze, bandages, needle, surgical thread, Novocain, and tetanus booster comes to a few dollars. Add in the technician's salary and the overhead for a clinic, and getting that arm stitched up should cost only $40 or $50, tops.

Legal barriers are the immediate reason such clinics are so rare, but why use one even if they are available—as long as you aren't paying for it or are on the hook for only a minor co-pay? Why go to a medical technician when you can see a physician? If, instead, patients had to look at a difference measured in hundreds of dollars out of their own pockets, the inexpensive clinic staffed by medical technicians would suddenly be attractive—and such medical clinics spring up like McDonald's wherever they are given a chance to do so.[17]

Example #2: Just-to-be-sure medicine. You turn 60 years old. You have high cholesterol and wonder whether you have clogged arteries. You visit a cardiologist, who gives you a stress test that reveals a few minor anomalies. He offers you the choice between a further test that would tell you a lot but leave some uncertainty, or a much more expensive procedure that gives a definitive answer. You choose the expensive one because, as long as the insurance company is paying for it, why not be sure? The bill is more than $10,000. You are happy to learn that your heart is in terrific shape. But there was nothing wrong to begin with.

If it had been a question of paying the bill yourself, you might have just gotten serious about your diet and exercise and not gone to see the cardiologist at all. If you had seen the cardiologist, you probably would have been satisfied with the less expensive diagnostic option.

Example #3. End-of-life care. Health care at the end of life—the phrase has become so much a term of art that it is often denoted by the acronym EOL—involves the last few weeks or months when a disease is either terminal or so serious in a person of advanced age that the chances of recovery are negligible. As the ability of medical science to keep people alive progressed during the last half of the twentieth century, the costs of EOL care soared. When I wrote the original edition of *In Our Hands*, they accounted for about 27 percent of the Medicare budget, a proportion that has remained about constant since then.[18] This is one of the least cost-effective ways of using limited government resources, and one of the least beneficial ways of using limited health care resources.

Now imagine a world in which your health care in old age is not provided by Medicare, but by an insurance policy that you choose as a supplement to your required catastrophic health insurance. You are given two choices: Policy A will provide full coverage for EOL care, whatever it involves. Policy B has a variety of clauses that, in effect, say that if you have disease from which you cannot recover, the insurance will pay for palliative and hospice care, but not for hospitalization and long-shot experimental therapies. The difference in the cost of the two policies over the course of years of payments will be thousands of dollars.

Perhaps you decide to choose the restricted policy, even though you are aware that you may have signed away a few months of earthly existence in exchange for more money to spend now. You have made a voluntary choice about your own medical care as you approach death—but you have made it, not a government rationing system. Perhaps you pay the extra costs for unlimited EOL care. But you will be paying for it, and the insurance rates will have been set to ensure that. The government is no longer in the position of requiring itself to pay tens of billions of dollars annually for EOL care.

Three Reforms for Approaching the Desired End State

Three reforms will go a long way toward enabling people to meet their health care needs the same way that they manage to keep their cars on the road. None requires a large bureaucracy to administer it.

1. Legally obligate medical insurers to treat the national population as a single pool.

2. Treat the value of employer-provided medical insurance as taxable income.

3. Reform tort law so it becomes easy to write legally binding waivers and restrictions on liability.

Legally Obligate Medical Insurers to Treat the National Population as a Single Pool. The Affordable Care Act has already taken a step forward on this reform by prohibiting insurers from denying coverage due to pre-existing conditions and requiring (with caveats) insurers to offer the same premium price to all applicants of the same age in the same geographic area. I propose a more sweeping reform that would be feasible only if the UBI exists, and that would apply both to the compulsory catastrophic health insurance and to supplemental insurance plans that people might voluntarily choose to buy: Insurance companies would be permitted to sell their insurance policies throughout the country, but they would be required to incorporate the population-wide incidence of all diseases and disabilities into their insurance rates and to offer the same rate for the same package of coverage to everyone the same age, whether they are purchasing the policy as individuals or as part of a group.[19] In other words, you would be able to buy a given insurance package for the same price as everyone else even if one of your parents had multiple sclerosis or you were paralyzed in an auto accident as a child. The only permissible differentiation in costs would be geographic (people in Tallahassee would not need to buy insurance based on prevailing medical costs in Los Angeles).

There is no unfairness in this for diseases and accidents that are not the fault of the victim. None of us "deserves" our genes, be they good or bad. None of us "deserves" to have been in the car safely ahead of a tractor-trailer truck that fishtails out of control and injures the people who in no way "deserved" to be in the car behind it.

A certain amount of unfairness is a cost of this reform when people voluntary do things that cause diseases and accidents. The implementation of the single-pool rule could try to mitigate this unfairness by allowing insurance companies to charge smokers and hang gliders more than people who do not smoke or hang glide. But the line between personal choice and pre-existing conditions can be fuzzy. (Obesity is an example.) It may well turn out that no-fault health insurance makes economic sense in the same way that no-fault car insurance has made sense. If the cost to the rest of us of subsidizing the health risks of smoking hang gliders is only a few dollars per year per person, the simplest solution for insurance companies and customers alike would be to throw the personal-responsibility health risks into the one-pool pot along with other kinds of health risks. I will leave those calculations to the health care specialists, observing simply that the requirement to treat the population as a single insurance pool is worth some residual unfairness if it eliminates the cosmic unfairness through which some people have genes or accidents that produce debilitation, pain, and physical handicaps that the rest of us are spared, through no fault or merit of anyone.

To make this work requires a trade-off, which brings me to the UBI's stipulation that everyone, starting at age 21, must use part of their grant to buy insurance that provides coverage for catastrophic or long-term health care needs. People would also be free to buy, and employers would be free to provide, health insurance that covers supplementary health care needs. But everyone would be required to buy the catastrophic policy.

The catastrophic policy would have a constant premium (adjusted for inflation) throughout the life span, in effect requiring young people to subsidize their older selves. I'm not talking about Ponzi schemes like Social Security or Medicare, which take money from the current crop of young people to pay for the benefits for the current crop of old people. What I have in mind are insurance policies owned by the individual, costing a monthly premium that the insurance company can afford to offer only if it is actuarially sound in the same way that life insurance rates must be actuarially sound. Insurance companies can make a profit selling life insurance to 20-somethings cheaply, even though they know that the all of their customers will eventually die. The same approach can ensure that people reach old age able to still pay an affordable rate for insurance.

Think of it this way: Suppose you start putting $3,000 a year into catastrophic health insurance at age 21, don't have need for it for 40 years, and then require a heart transplant. If the insurance company has made 6 percent annually on your premiums over those 40 years (a reasonable expectation—see Chapter 4), it will have accrued about $498,000. Add in all the people who don't need it until their seventies or eighties, when the value of their accrued premiums will be in the millions, and you can see what I mean by "requiring young people to subsidize their older selves." Then add all the people who die without ever having a need for catastrophic or long-term care, or whose lifetime claims are far below the accrued value of their premiums, and you can see why a low constant premium over the life span is feasible if everybody is starting at 21.

I chose $3,000, meaning a monthly premium of $250, as an estimate of the cost of catastrophic health insurance. Estimating is unavoidable—there is nothing remotely similar to the kind of scenario I present (universal entry into the catastrophic health care insurance at age 21, with a constant real premium for life) in today's insurance marketplace. But consider the plans eligible for purchase under the Affordable Care Act, which provide general coverage, not just catastrophic insurance.[20] The median monthly payment for such plans, running from Bronze through Platinum, for someone age 21 is $216; for someone 31, $252. Perhaps the most surprising is the median cost for someone 61, just a few years from being eligible for Medicare: $624. My thought is that if an insurance company can make a profit from a $624 monthly premium paid by someone who is highly likely to experience significant needs for health care, it seems plausible that they could charge that 61-year-old $250 for catastrophic health insurance if that person had already been paying that that premium every month for 40 years.

I do not insist on precisely $3,000. The sense of the proposition is this: Figure out the cost of an insurance policy that would pay for extraordinary health care costs, including major surgery and illnesses involving long-term care, when the entire population is a single pool. That is the amount of money that I am willing for the government to provide as part of the UBI. If it is discovered that the right number is $3,800, then the nation can afford to set the annual grant at $13,800. The arguments in the rest of the book assume $10,000 remains after health care is deducted. As long as this amount remains constant, the amount devoted to health care is irrelevant to those arguments. Under any plausible assumptions about the add-on to $3,000, the UBI would probably still be cheaper than the current system in 2016 and far cheaper than the current system by 2020.

Treat the Value of Employer-Provided Medical Insurance as Taxable Income. The overarching purpose of the reforms is to have the people who consume the health care be the same people who pay for the health care. Employer-provided health insurance is one of the biggest obstacles to making that happen. The way to get rid of that obstacle is to treat employer-provided insurance as taxable income. Under the existing system, people with employer-provided insurance are getting a government subsidy equal to their marginal income tax rate (federal and state combined). Hence reform #2. Take away that subsidy by treating medical benefits as taxable income. This reform says to the employee: "Your medical benefit is worth X dollars, and you're going to pay income tax on that money. Would you rather have the cash instead?" If your company has provided precisely the coverage you want, you are indifferent because you would end up paying the same amount for the same coverage if you bought individual insurance. But if you can get insurance that satisfies your personal preferences for less money, you have an incentive to take the cash and buy your own insurance.[21]

The first two reforms combined produce an insurance industry that sells a product to individuals who are looking for the right product for the lowest price—the crucial missing ingredient in the current market for health care.

Reform Tort Law So It Becomes Easy to Write Legally Binding Waivers and Restrictions on Liability. Earlier, I said that low-cost medical clinics would proliferate like McDonald's franchises if they were given a chance. One of the things I had in mind by "given a chance" was the repeal of licensing laws that support a medical cartel.[22] But even if licensing laws are repealed, the second half of this reform is essential. Under today's tort jurisprudence, the neighborhood clinic I envisioned cannot have a piece of paper for you to sign when you walk in that says, in legally binding language, "We do minor medical repairs here. You can sue us if the arm we sew up becomes infected because we failed to sterilize our instruments, but not if you suffer a reaction from some exotic allergy." In the absence of such contracts, cheap medical care is impossible because everything involving medical care is subject to strict legal scrutiny and large jury awards. Under the current system, it is as if you were not permitted to open a diner unless you hired a cook who has passed a master chef's exam. The costs this imposes on the system are enormous and needless. A great many medical tasks are the health profession's equivalent of cooking hamburgers.

This reform also addresses malpractice. The effects of jury awards for punitive damages are well publicized. In some especially vulnerable specialties, such as obstetrics, malpractice insurance has become so expensive that large numbers of practitioners are leaving the field altogether. Malpractice awards add just as importantly to the bottom line for the consumer by inducing

Evolving Standards

You wouldn't need to negotiate a contract every time you visited a health care provider. Freedom to write binding contracts for medical services would quickly lead to some standard contracts that almost everybody would use. Their virtue is that they would be sensible. Most health care providers don't want or expect to be freed from responsibility for incompetence. Most patients don't (before the fact) expect health care providers to practice their craft with godlike perfection. A market for contracts will lead consumers and practitioners to converge on a few good ones that correspond with common sense and good faith.

Guarantees for new products provide an analogous case. Even without a law requiring it, almost all the products we buy are backed by guarantees that consumers find acceptable without having to negotiate them on a case-by-case basis. Successful health care providers will figure out how to offer service agreements that meet the same demand of the market, and yet are ones that they can live with.

Why not have the government decide on reasonable standards? Because the government won't. It will be captive to the National Association of Trial Lawyers and the American Medical Association. If you want reasonable standards to evolve, let consumers who want affordable but competent health care come to their own agreements with health care providers who seek their business.

physicians to practice defensive medicine.[23] Many legislative solutions have been tried but with only modest success. The solution is to make waivers and restrictions easy and binding.

Genuinely Affordable Health Care

The effects of these reforms will be to flatten the overall increases in health care costs overall and drive down the cost of routine health care. This is not wishful thinking, but a straightforward consequence of changing the forces that currently affect the price of health care.

The first and inevitable effect is that millions of consumers will shift toward the desired end state as I expressed it earlier: paying for regular health care out of pocket and insuring against catastrophe. More formally, people will shift to supplementary policies (in addition to the required catastrophic health insurance) with high deductibles, or perhaps to no coverage at all for routine care. The millions of people who have done that will become active consumers of inexpensive care for routine health problems, at the same time that the reform of tort law has permitted health care providers to enter into limited-liability agreements with their customers. The market for, and then supply of, small, inexpensive clinics will expand, becoming a major part of the health care system.

Putting numbers on the cost of health care under these circumstances is a matter of guesswork, but this much is sure: Costs will drop substantially. When health care is subjected to the same choices that people make about everything else in their lives—"Is it worth it to me?"—the health care industry will respond in the same way as other industries constrained by market forces, with better products at lower cost.

4

Retirement

When it comes to providing for comfortable retirements, the UBI is superior to Social Security for everyone from the richest to the poorest.

Start with the poorest. Most people are aware that Social Security is a bad deal as an investment, but a widespread impression persists that at least Social Security provides a floor for everyone that has nearly eliminated poverty among the elderly. Social Security does not accomplish even that much. As of 2014, 4.6 million elderly Americans were below the poverty line— 1 out of every 10 people age 65 and older.[24]

Social Security can leave so many people so poor because it is not universal and because the benefits for people who have worked only a portion of their adult lives are well below the poverty line. To qualify for Social Security benefits on your own, you must have worked in jobs covered by Social Security for at least 10 years. Many people do not meet that basic requirement and must qualify indirectly through a spouse's benefits. Many cannot do that. For example, consider the situation that faces a woman who has had two or three marriages, none of which lasted 10 years, or has been in long-term cohabitations, and spent her adult life as a full-time mother and housewife. She gets no survivor benefits via a divorced husband's employment record unless the marriage lasted 10 years and she has not remarried. She gets no benefits on her own unless she has worked 10 years or more.[25] Such a woman can reach 66 with no retirement income whatsoever. Add in the men who have not met the 10-year employment requirement, and you can explain why 20 percent of 67-year-olds in the bottom income quintile receive no Social Security at all.[26] Many more who have worked sporadically over their lives qualify for benefits too low to keep them out of poverty in old age.[27] Thus the first significant advantage of the UBI over the current system is that it is universal, and even in the worst case provides $10,000 a year in cash for every elderly person in the country.

The Range of Expectations

But the UBI does more than give everyone a guaranteed income floor. The UBI makes it possible for ordinary people, including poor ones, to have not just a livable retirement but a comfortable one. Take the case of a man who has retired at age 66 at the beginning of 2015 after working steadily for 45 years at low-income jobs all his life—making the equivalent, let us say, of $15,000 in 2014 dollars every year.[28] If you go to the Social Security Administration's web page for calculating benefits and enter those assumptions, you will be told that he will get a monthly Social Security payment of $916, or an annual income of $10,992. That is $362 below the poverty line for someone 65 or older living in a one-person household as of 2015.[29]

That meager Social Security benefit will have been created by 45 years of payroll tax payments—money taken directly from the employee's salary and diverted from the salary pool indirectly by the employer's required "contribution." As of 2015, the amount of that payment for a man making $15,000 was $1,860 annually.[30] Now suppose that for 45 years the government had been putting those contributions into an index-based mutual fund owned by the low-income worker.

During the period from 1970 to 2014, the years in which the rate of return to the S&P 500 apples to our hypothetical low-income worker, the real annualized return[31] was 6.1 percent. It was a typical 45-year period. Analysts routinely have assumed real annualized returns averaging 6 to 7 percent—as with the expectation of a 7 percent return used by the Advisory Council to the Social Security Administration (SSA) in 1994–96, the 6.5 percent expectation used by the SSA in analyzing the three models for modifying Social Security that were presented to the President's Commission to Strengthen Social Security in 2001, and the 6.8 percent used by the Congressional Budget Office in analyzing the work of the commission.[32]

Given a 6.1 percent return compounded monthly and an annual contribution of an additional $1,860, our worker would have accumulated about $441,000 by the end of 2014. If you go to an annuities calculator webpage, you will be told that our low-income worker would have been able to buy a lifetime annuity paying $30,264 per year, almost three times the amount that same worker gets under Social Security.[33]

But in making the case for a UBI, I need a margin of safety. So let me introduce the assumption that the average annualized return over a person's work life will be just 4 percent, treating that as the worst-case scenario.

In this scenario, the UBI has been put in place. The young man making $15,000 a year puts $1,860 of the $10,000 into an index fund for 45 years. With a 4 percent return, the accumulation will be just $234,000. But that will buy an annuity worth $16,056. In addition, he will continue to get $10,000 cash from the UBI. The total works out to an annual income of $26,056 under the UBI compared with Social Security's $10,992. Given all we know about markets and risk, a 4 percent average real annualized return really is a worst-case scenario. Over the course of American history, an investor who left his money alone for three or four decades could not fail to make a substantial profit if he invested in a broad-based portfolio of stocks. Let us apply the story from this chart to my worst-case scenario. The next figure shows the average compound average growth rate (CAGR) over every 45-year period from 1871–1915 to 1970–2014.

Figure 4-1. 45-Year Compound Average Growth Rate for the Stock Market, 1871–2014

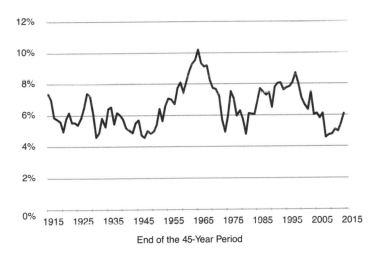

End of the 45-Year Period

Source: Figures calculated using the CAGR calculator at www.moneychimp.com/features/ market_cagr.htm, based on the data downloaded from Robert Shiller, "Online Data," www.econ. yale.edu/~shiller/data.htm.

The CAGR over a 45-year period was above 6 percent in 60 of the 100 periods of 45 years and fell below 5 percent in only 14 of them. The CAGR in the most recent period, 1970–2014, was 6.1 percent.

But when talking about retirement, the issue for many people is not averages. People are worried about worst cases. Most recently, the stock market plunge in 2008 and 2009 provided politicians and editorial writers with new material for attacking plans to privatize Social Security.

The figure lends perspective. Suppose, for example, that you were unlucky enough to have invested every cent of your retirement nest egg at the peak of the market in 1929 before the Great Depression. As your 45-year period ended in 1973, whatever you put in would have increased in value more than eightfold—a CAGR of about 5.7 percent. Or suppose that you had suffered the unluckiest timing in the graph: Your baseline year was 1887, you invested all of your money in that year, and you had to withdraw it to buy your retirement annuity in 1931 at the bottom of the Great Depression. In that case, your nest egg would have grown about sevenfold and your average return would still have been about 4.6 percent. Or we may take the data all the way back to 1801, the baseline year of economist Jeremy Siegel's reconstruction of total real returns for the US stock market.[34] None of the 45-year periods for the first three-quarters of the nineteenth century had a growth rate as low as 4 percent. My estimated 4 percent annual real return over 45 years assumes that everyone's timing under the UBI will always be worse than the unluckiest long-term investors in American history.

Frequently Raised Objections

No matter how decisive the data on long-term returns from the stock market may be, many readers will not like the idea of letting people manage their own retirement plans without the backstop of Social Security. Here are my responses to the most common objections I have heard.

"Many people won't put anything away or will invest their money foolishly." A familiar argument for preferring Social Security to a privatized version is that Social Security ensures an income floor for everyone, no matter how improvident or how incompetent an investor a person might be. They are wrong about "everyone," as I discussed at the opening of the chapter—Social Security leaves many people behind. More to the point of this question, *the UBI does provide a universal floor.* Everyone, including the improvident and incompetent who have squandered everything, still have $10,000 discretionary income a year each, $20,000 for a couple, no matter what. Four people who have completely squandered everything can pool their resources and have $40,000 per year, and so on. If a guaranteed floor is important to you, the UBI does a far better job than the current system.

But squandering everything is extreme. The broader question is whether ordinary people can be expected to plan for their own retirements and invest their money wisely, to which my short answer is: Why not? The large retirement income that I produced from a working income of $15,000 a year is based on the same amount that people at that income level are currently required by law to save for retirement. Accumulating that sum does not require people to make sophisticated investment choices; it is based on the result if they buy a fund based on a broad market index and leave it alone during a hypothesized worst investment period in American history. For that matter, obtaining a 4 percent return does not require investing exclusively in equities. The CBO analysis of the President's Commission to Strengthen Social Security projects an average real return of 5.2 percent from a portfolio consisting of 50 percent equities, 20 percent treasury bonds, and 30 percent corporate bonds.[35]

The question then becomes, how many people will take advantage of this easily available strategy? There is one simple solution: Require everyone to take advantage of it. If the only reason you oppose the UBI is that you are worried about people doing foolish things with their money, continue the legal compulsion and restrict the investment choices. The UBI could be modified to stipulate that some percentage of the grant be deposited in a retirement account of diversified stocks and bonds.

But before you choose that option, think for a moment about a world in which such compulsion does not exist, but everyone knows that they must provide for their own retirement if they want more than $10,000 a year. Today, many low-income people have never heard of diversification and long-term gains because they have never had any money to invest and no need to plan for their own retirement. In the world of the UBI, talk about investments will be part of the morning conversations over coffee in small-town cafes and after work in blue-collar taverns. Part of that conversation will consist of wild-eyed schemes—but most of it will consist of the others ridiculing the dreamer, because the principle of diversification will have become common knowledge. You won't have to be a genius or have connections on Wall Street to invest your retirement savings sensibly.

Of course there will be people who make decisions that you consider imprudent, but ask yourself why they should not be allowed to do so. Think of it this way: More than 32,000 people were killed in automobile accidents in 2014.[36] The harm they suffer is not nearly as benign as having a lower retirement income than they could have enjoyed if they had behaved differently. They are dead. More than 2 million people were injured in automobile accidents in 2014. Many of them are severely disabled for the rest of their lives, another penalty far more devastating than a loss of retirement income. Yet we permit anyone to drive who can pass a simple driving test that does nothing to measure the applicant's impulsiveness, drinking or drug habits, intelligence, or judgment. For that matter, it does not even test his ability to drive except in the simplest conditions. A more thorough screening process to select qualified drivers is economically and technically feasible. By installing it, and consequently denying driving privileges to a substantial proportion of the American population, we could save thousands of lives per year. Given what is known about the relationship of the problematic driving traits to socioeconomic factors, we must expect the people who would be denied driving privileges to be disproportionately poor and disadvantaged.[37]

Do you favor such a policy? If not, then it's useful to think about why you (like me) are willing to countenance tens of thousands of deaths and millions of injuries per year in the name of the freedom to drive. Having answered that question for yourself, you should then ask why it is okay to tell people who are not clinically retarded or mentally ill that, for their own good and that of society as a whole, they should not be permitted to use the grant as they see fit.

A UBI option that mandated contributions to a retirement fund is an option I could live with, but I hope to persuade you by the end of the book that it is inferior to a society in which people are free to make their own choices, including their own mistakes. The summary statement of the argument to come is this: A UBI with compulsory retirement saving will reduce the number of people who completely fritter away their retirement savings. But it will also reduce the ability of people to pursue their dreams for how to live their lives. Under a system where even the most foolish or the most unlucky will still have $10,000 a year until they die, and in a society that once again has a vital set of civic institutions to deal with misfortune, no one is going to starve in the streets. The greater freedom to do wonderful things with one's life is worth the greater freedom to make mistakes.

"The stock market is inherently risky. People need the security of a government guarantee." You have probably encountered an argument in the debate over proposals to privatize part of Social Security that goes something like this: "How can we rest the security of our elderly population on the vagaries of the stock market? No matter what the history of investments has been, we cannot be sure that the future will produce the same results. Better to maintain a system in which the government guarantees the result."[38]

In the specific case of the UBI, a guarantee of $10,000 a year remains. But the larger fallacy in that argument needs to be more widely recognized. *If stocks do not continue to appreciate in real value by an average of 4 percent over the next 45 years, the government will not be able to make good on its current promises anyway.* All of the government's promises depend on economic growth at least as robust as that implied by an anemic 4 percent average return in the stock market. If we institute the UBI and the next generation happens upon a 45-year period so catastrophic that their retirement fund goes bust, the current system will have gone bust as well. Here is the difference between the risks of the current system and the UBI. If you own your retirement account, you can make your own decisions about how to protect against the prospect of hard times. If your retirement remains with the government, you must trust politicians to foresee hard times and act wisely.

The main points to remember in thinking about the UBI and retirement are:

- The UBI guarantees the universal income floor that the current system does not.

- The 4 percent assumption is conservative—and it produces a far larger retirement income than the current system, even for low-income workers.

- Trusting in the growth of the American economy is not a choice. The risks of the UBI are no greater than the risks of the current system.

5

Poverty

The topic of this chapter is poverty, with *poverty* defined as the lack of means to provide for basic material needs and comforts. I conceive of poverty along a dimension ranging from purely involuntary to purely voluntary. Involuntary poverty occurs when someone who plays by the rules is still poor. Voluntary poverty occurs when someone fritters away resources and opportunities through idleness, fecklessness, or vice.

The End of Involuntary Poverty

The UBI lowers the rate of involuntary poverty to zero for everyone who has any capacity to work or any capacity to get along with other people—which means just about everybody. In a world where every adult starts with $10,000 a year, none of these people needs to go without decent food, shelter, or clothing. No one needs to do without most of the amenities of life, even when *amenities* is broadly defined. This statement holds even after taking the expenses of retirement and medical care into account. Here is the arithmetic, if we use the official poverty line as the definition for poverty:

The Working-Aged. The UBI gives every adult catastrophic health insurance and $10,000 in cash per year. Throughout the rest of discussion of the working-aged, I am going to assume that everyone is farsighted and puts $2,000 per year into a retirement fund, leaving the recipient with $8,000 left help him stay above the poverty line. In other words, every conclusion that follows has a $2,000 cushion, if we are asking whether a working-age person has an income above the poverty line from year to year before retirement.

An individual living alone needs to work—but not very much even at a minimum-wage job. The official definition of poverty in 2014 meant an income of less than $12,316 for an unrelated individual under the age of

65. Working 49 weeks for 40 hours a week at the minimum wage of $7.25 an hour produces $14,210. Combine that with the $8,000 not used for the retirement fund and medical insurance, and the total income of $22,210 amounts to 1.8 times the poverty threshold. The economy is bad? Someone could be out of work for 37 weeks and still reach the poverty threshold by working at a minimum-wage job and UBI—even after setting aside $2,000 for retirement. For a couple without children, the poverty threshold in 2014 was $15,853. They could both be putting away $2,000 for retirement, and the remaining cash would lift them above the poverty line with neither one of them working at all.

There are children to worry about? The poverty line for a couple with one child under 18 was $16,317 in 2014. If the mother stays home and the father works 49 weeks at a minimum-wage job, the combined income of the parents after contributions to retirement and health care would be $14,210 from the job plus $16,000 from the two grants, or a $30,210 family income, 1.9 times the poverty line. The economy is bad? The couple can work a grand total of just one week out of the year at a minimum-wage job and reach the poverty line.

I could extend the examples, but the point should be clear: Surpassing the official poverty line under the UBI is easy for working-age people in a wide range of living circumstances, even in a bad economy, even assuming jobs at the rock-bottom wage, and even assuming that $2,000 is being tucked away in a retirement fund. To see how unrealistically stringent these conditions are, consider that the minimum wage I have been using is $7.25 an hour. The average janitor earns two-thirds more than that—$12.24 an hour in 2014.[39] Under the UBI, the average janitor working 40 hours a week for 49 weeks a year would have a total disposable income of $31,990 even if he is putting away $2,000 for retirement.

The Elderly. The elderly who have been putting aside $2,000 a year through-out their working lives need do nothing to stay out of poverty once they reach retirement age, as demonstrated in the last chapter with a smaller annual contribution of $1,860. With a $2,000 contribution and the standard assumption of a 4 percent return, an individual's retirement fund at age 67 will be about $252,000, sufficient to purchase a lifetime annuity paying $17,292 annually. Adding in $10,000 from the continuing grant (no longer having to deduct $2,000 for retirement), the annual cash income of a single person upon retiring will be about $27,000, or $54,000 for a couple. The grant plus annuity from the retirement savings puts an elderly individual living alone at 2.4 times the poverty line and an elderly couple at 3.8 times the poverty line.

Even for the elderly who have put nothing aside whatsoever for their retirement, the only thing needed to stay above the official poverty line is to find someone else to live with. Together, they will have $20,000 a year, well above the $14,326 that was the 2014 official poverty line for a two-person household with the householder 65 or older. To be below the poverty line requires that a person to have saved nothing for retirement and to be unable to find anyone to share expenses. In that case, the $10,000 cash from the UBI will be less than the $11,354 official poverty for someone age 65 or older living alone. Does that constitute involuntary poverty? People will answer that question differently. My own answer is given at the end of the chapter.

Frequently Raised Objections

Four objections to the foregoing discussion may be raised: Using the official poverty line is too ungenerous a standard. I haven't considered the value of the present set of welfare programs available to low-income people that would be lost under the UBI. What about poor young adults under 21 who are not eligible for the grant? Who will care for those people who cannot work at all?

"The official poverty line is too stingy." The official poverty line has only the fuzziest relation to actual poverty.[40] Let us assume for purposes of argument that it is too stingy, and substitute the definition of poverty adopted by European social democrats, an income of less than half the national median income. Instead of using median income for the entire population, I will use the tougher standard of median earnings of full-time, year-round workers as the basis. In 2014, that number was $46,922, half of which is $23,461.[41]

Coincidentally (I did not not choose the size of the UBI to produce this result), this demanding social-democratic definition of "being out of poverty" is within a few hundred dollars of the amount ($23,080) obtained from work and the UBI by an unattached individual who works a minimum-wage job for 40 hour a weeks 52 weeks a year *even putting aside $2,000 for retirement*. If the average janitor is the person in question, he would escape poverty by the social democrats' definition with just 32 weeks of work. The UBI makes it easy for most people to escape poverty even under poverty's most liberal definition.

"For some poor people, the current system is better." Under the UBI, many programs to help the poor would be gone: the earned income tax credit (EITC), Temporary Assistance for Needy Families (TANF), Supplemental Nutrition Assistance Program (SNAP, formerly known as food stamps), Medicaid, housing subsidies, and the other programs listed in Appendix A. In net, which poor people would benefit under the UBI? Who would lose more than they gain?

If you're working-age and don't have children, it's not even close. You get extremely little under the current system. A single person making $12,000 a year gets an EITC of just $150 and maximum annual SNAP benefits of about $696.[42] For a person with no income at all, the maximum food stamp allowance is about $2,328. That's it, except for in-kind services that vary from place to place. (TANF is available only for people with children.) The UBI of $10,000 plus catastrophic health insurance is vastly better.

All low-income married or cohabiting couples with children in which at least one person works for a substantial portion of the year are better off under the UBI than under the current system. This is true everywhere in the nation. Consider New York, one of the highest-benefit states, and the situation of a couple with one child in which the man earns $12,000, less than the minimum wage for a full-time job, and the woman doesn't work at all.[43] Under the current system, this married family of three gets $3,250 in EITC, a New York state earned income credit of $951, and about $4,500 in food stamps—a total of $8,701 in cash or cash-like benefits. The family is also probably eligible for the Weatherization Assistance Program, Home Energy Assistance Program, Medicaid, School Meals, and Summer Meals.[44] The UBI gives that same couple a package worth $20,000 plus catastrophic health insurance—not a close comparison, no matter how those other benefits are valued.

If neither the man nor the woman in a two-adult family works at all—an extreme case—the UBI is better for couples everywhere except the highest-benefit states, and even there it is a close call. In 2014, a New York couple with one child in which neither partner worked at all got about $9,240 in cash from TANF and about $6,132 from food stamps, totaling $15,372, plus other in-kind benefits. The total value of those benefits might exceed $20,000, depending on how the in-kind benefits are valued, but not by much. In less generous states, even couples who don't work at all are better off under the UBI.

The one major category of people who would get the grant but are better off financially under the current system is single parents who have no earnings and are caring for more than one child. In New York, a single parent caring for two children can get a maximum of $13,308 per year from TANF and SNAP combined, plus Medicaid and other in-kind benefits.[45] Everywhere in the country, even in most of the low-benefit states, a case can be made that the total value of their benefits package is greater than the UBI. Theoretically, the UBI does not become clearly preferable for such women until earnings exceed $15,000 to $20,000, depending on the number of children and the state. I say "theoretically" because, under the current system, many women who qualify for benefits of this magnitude do not actually get them. (Many who legally qualify do not apply.) In contrast, all single mothers will get the full $10,000 plus catastrophic medical insurance under the UBI.

I should also note that single mothers under the UBI do not need to live in poverty. First, they have the choice to work. If they work most of the year at a minimum-wage job, their earnings plus the grant get them out of poverty. In addition, a woman living under the UBI can get child support that is often unavailable under the current system—the father of her child has a monthly income arriving at a known bank account that can be tapped, and modern DNA analysis makes identification of the biological father easy (see Chapter 6 for more on this).

But the greater availability of child support is only one of many new possibilities a single mother has for coping with her situation under the UBI. Even if a woman decides not to work but has $10,000 in cash to bring to the table, she can find some joint living arrangement with family or friends, or find some other group with whom to pool her resources. A single mother living in a world where she has the UBI, and so do her family and friends, has a variety of ways to avoid poverty—by her own choices and actions, not by the dispensation of a bureaucracy.

"What about poor young adults under 21 who are not eligible for the grant? Who will care for those people who cannot work at all?" I group these two questions because the answer to both is the same, and it extends the point I just made about single mothers over 21: *The key to understanding the effects of the UBI is not that it provides each individual adult with $10,000 per year, but that it provides all adults with $10,000 per year.* "In our hands" refers not only, nor even primarily, to "our hands" as individuals, but "our hands" as families, communities, and civil society as a whole. I discuss those who cannot work at all because of physical or mental incapacity in Chapter 11. I discuss people under the age of 21 in Chapter 6. The bottom line is this: Under the UBI, hardly anyone will be forced to live in poverty, compared with the 11 to 14 percent of the population that has been classified as poor in the United States for the last 30 years.

The fact that no able-bodied person *needs* to live in poverty doesn't mean that no one *will* live in poverty. Some people behave in ways that ensure they will live in squalor, will not have enough money to buy food, or will be evicted for not paying the rent. They may drink away their money or gamble it away. Some people will be feckless under any system. The UBI ends nearly all involuntary poverty—the kind that exists when people have done the ordinary things right and are still poor. These are the people who most deserve help. Under the UBI, their poverty is ended.

What Should Be Expected of People Who Have Had Tough Breaks?

Whether the paragraphs above are self-evidently true or unrealistically optimistic depends on one's premises about what human beings can be expected to do. Many observers on the left (and some on the right) argue that millions of people cannot be expected to go out and work at minimum-wage jobs or otherwise cope with daily life because of disadvantages they have suffered—racism, broken homes, poor education, poverty, and the like. I have just asserted that the number of people who cannot be expected to meet those standards is small.

I work from the premise that everyone not clinically retarded or mentally ill makes choices. Some people are able to make only the most basic choices, but one of those basic choices is whether to seek work and take it when offered. Another basic choice open to everyone is whether to behave cooperatively with family and neighbors. Conversely, failure to seek work or failure to behave cooperatively are choices. To deny that these are choices is to deny the humanity of the people we want to help.

6

The Underclass

The underclass denotes a class of people who exist at the margins of American society. They are usually poor, but poverty is a less important indicator than personal behavior destructive to themselves and to their communities. Membership in the underclass is not a yes/no proposition, but three categories of people are overrepresented in the underclass: never-married women with children, able-bodied young men who are out of the labor force, and chronic criminals.[46] How might the UBI affect them?

Never-Married Women with Children

The UBI is extremely likely to reduce births to single women and increase births to married women. Consider three categories of women in low-income communities: single women under 21, single women 21 and older, and married women of all ages.

Single Women Under 21. The UBI radically increases the economic penalty of having a baby for a single woman under 21, an age group that in 2014 accounted for about 28 percent of all births to single women.[47] She no longer gets any government assistance—no cash payment, no food stamps, no Medicaid, no housing subsidies, and no subsidies for day care.[48]

The UBI also increases the economic penalty on the parents of a teenage mother who is still living at home. At present, the net financial effect on her parents is offset by the stream of benefits that accompanies the baby. Under the UBI, the costs of the new baby will fall on the girl's parents (in low-income neighborhoods, typically just her mother). The incentives to pressure the daughter to avoid pregnancy will increase.

The UBI increases the likelihood that the father of the child faces an economic penalty. In today's low-income neighborhoods, having sex with many women confers social status on the male.[49] When a child results, many fathers pay nothing; others give minor support for a few years and then fade away.[50] Many states have passed legislation to make unmarried fathers pay child support, but such efforts confront a problem: Many of these fathers have no visible income, and enforcing child-support orders is difficult even when they do. Under the UBI, every man age 21 or older has $833 deposited to a known bank account every month. (In this and other calculations henceforth, I assume that $3,000 of the grant is allocated to health care and that retirement contributions are not mandatory.) Police do not need to track him down or try to find him on a day when he has cash on hand. All they need is a court order to tap the bank account. Even teenage fathers who are not yet getting the grant need not escape. Just write the child-support law so that their obligation accumulates until they turn 21. The state pays the child support until then, at which time his cash grant is tapped not only for the continuing child support but to pay back the money already spent.

In other words, *every party to the birth of a child to a single woman under the age of 21 suffers immediate and large increased costs under the UBI.* Many young women will take steps to avoid getting pregnant that they do not take now. Among those young women who do get pregnant, larger proportions will choose to give the baby up for adoption or to have an abortion.[51] The net effect will be a large reduction in the number of babies born to and raised by single teenage girls.

Single Women 21 and Older. Every unmarried woman over the age of 21 will have $10,000 to pay for the costs of a baby. This is somewhat less than the value of the package of benefits in an average state that a single mother gets now, but the reduced amount of benefits is not the main consideration.[52] The big difference is that, under the current system, the birth of a baby brings resources that would not be offered if the baby did not exist. Under the UBI, the baby will be a drain on resources. Consider the implications of this difference for women who want to have babies, women who don't want to have babies and who value having income to spend on themselves, and women who want to have babies, but also value income to spend on themselves.

Single women 21 and older who want to have babies. In many states, these women will get less under the UBI than under the current system and thereby will have some increased incentive to avoid pregnancy. But $10,000 is enough to enable them to do what they want to do anyway—have a baby—so I do not predict major changes in their fertility.

Single women 21 and older who do not want to have babies. These women have a substantial incentive to avoid getting pregnant under the UBI. Under the current system, a woman who does not want to get pregnant is at least compensated if she has a baby. Under the UBI, having a baby is pure economic loss.

Single women 21 and older who want to have babies but also value income to spend on themselves. For women in this category (probably a large majority of all single women), the response to the UBI will form a continuum. The less eager a woman is to have a baby, the greater the likelihood that under the UBI she will avoid getting pregnant. But any woman in this category experiences a major change in incentives. Under the current system, she is subsidized for doing something she wanted to do anyway. Under the UBI, she will have to bear a cost for doing the same thing.

I have framed the argument in the abstract, but it will not be abstract when the UBI goes into effect. Think in terms of a 20-year-old woman from a low-income neighborhood with a boyfriend. She knows she will start receiving a monthly deposit of $833 on her next birthday. She also knows women in her neighborhood who are already getting that deposit. The ones without babies are spending it on themselves. Her friends with babies are buying diapers and baby food, and probably living with their mothers because they cannot afford a place of their own. Under the UBI, the opportunity costs of having a baby will be obvious and alarming to low-income young women in the same way that they have always been obvious and alarming to middle-class and affluent young women.

Married Women. Almost all young married couples want to have children eventually. Some of those couples defer having a child or limit the number of children for economic reasons. The low-income portion of that group will have $10,000 in additional family income under the UBI as soon as one partner is over 21 and $20,000 when both of them are over 21. In both cases, the UBI makes a first child or an additional child financially more feasible. There is no counterbalancing group for which the UBI makes having children less attractive. It seems to be a sure bet that births to low-income and working-class married couples will go up. The reason this is important to the underclass is that it increases the availability of role models for young men in poor neighborhoods. It is possible to grow up in some inner-city neighborhoods without ever knowing a man who acts as a good father to his children and a good husband to his wife. Increasing the number of such visible men is arguably as important as reducing the number of births to single women.[53]

Able-Bodied Young Males Not in the Labor Market

The second population of people who embody the underclass consists of able-bodied young men in low-income neighborhoods who do not work or even look for work. Through the middle of the twentieth century, such young males were rare. Since the middle of the 1960s, they have become common. Initially, dropout from the labor force was most conspicuous among young black males, but more recently the dropout among young white males has also been substantial. As of 2014, among males ages 18 to 25, not in school and with no more than a high school education, 17 percent were not even looking for work—more than one out of six.[54]

Some of these men live with parents. Some live with girlfriends. Many have income, but not from regular jobs. The money may come from crime, the gray market, or sporadic daywork. How will the UBI affect their behavior after they turn 21?

One possibility is that the UBI's work disincentives will increase the number of young men and young women who leave the labor market. That worry is not restricted to the underclass but to everyone, and requires a chapter of its own (the next one). For now, I am talking exclusively about young men over 21 who already have dropped out of the labor market even without the UBI.

The UBI complicates their lives. It forces them to have an income, and one that other people know about. That fact produces a cascading set of consequences through what I call *the Doolittle Effect*, for reasons explained in the text box.

Consider first the young men who have persuaded parents or girlfriends to provide them with a place to live and food. The UBI goes into effect.

George Bernard Shaw's Version of the UBI

In *Pygmalion* and later in *My Fair Lady*, Alfred P. Doolittle is an able-bodied man often out of the labor force who fathered Eliza without marrying her mother. Then Henry Higgins recommends him as the most original moralist in England, and Alfred is consequently willed a large income by an American businessman. Here is the *My Fair Lady* version of Alfred's lament about his changed situation:

> I was happy. I was free. I touched pretty nigh everyone for money when I wanted it, same as I touched him [Henry Higgins]. Now I'm tied neck and heels and everybody touches me. A year ago I hadn't a relation in the world except one or two who wouldn't speak to me. Now I've fifty, and not a decent week's wages among the lot of them. I have to live for others now, not for myself. Middle-class morality.

Eliza suggests that Doolittle could just give back the money if that's the way he feels about it. Doolittle replies, "That's the tragedy of it, Eliza. It's easy to say chuck it, but I haven't the nerve. We're all intimidated. That's what we are, intimidated."[55]

Thus the Doolittle Effect.

Suddenly, both parents and girlfriends know that their lodger has $833 being deposited into a bank account every month. For most parents and girlfriends, the situation will now have changed materially.

Some of these young men will be kicked out. They were allowed to live in the house or apartment on sufferance because they claimed to have no other options. Now they undeniably have options. Other men will find that the parent or girlfriend now insists on receiving a portion of the $833. The man faces a monetary price for his lifestyle that did not previously exist.

Furthermore, that price is constantly subject to an increase: When the sponsoring parent or girlfriend runs into a financial shortfall, he will be asked to help out. Before, the young man had a claim on their support. Now, the parent or girlfriend has a claim on the young man.

The incentives for this young man to get a job will also have changed. Let's say that he could get a low-wage job netting him $1,000 a month. Under the current system, he would be pressured to spend a large part of that $1,000 on the housing and food that he had been getting for nothing. If he moved out, almost all of the $1,000 in earned income would be eaten up by those costs. A full-time job would provide only a few hundred dollars' difference in discretionary income. Moving out and working is unattractive. He stays put—rationally, in the short term.

The UBI gives him an income stream. Large numbers of these young men will find themselves forced to pay for rent and food. The only choice open to a man who finds himself under that pressure is to pay the girlfriend or parent or find his own place and buy his own food. Some men like living with the parents or girlfriend and do not move. But for those who prefer a place of their own, taking a job now makes economic sense.

To take a simple example, suppose that the man finds himself having to pay exactly $833 per month for food and rent to a girlfriend. Under the UBI, a $1,000-per-month job provides him with $1,000 in additional discretionary income. It will not often be that simple in practice, but the principle generalizes: A man who has been living off others but would rather live on his own and then acquires an income stream will typically find that it has become rational to move out if he works. He has gone from a situation in which he had little incentive to work to a situation in which he has substantial incentive to work.

It is hard to say whether the Doolittle Effect will include pressure to marry the mother of his child. In an age when cohabitation has become common, perhaps not, especially in states where child support can be enforced as easily against men who have never married the mother as against those who did (see Chapter 10). But pressures to act like a father will probably increase. A man with a steady income, as every man will have under the UBI, is treated differently from a man without a steady income. The fact of his income gives him a standing in others' calculations, including the assumption that a man can be pushed to shoulder responsibilities.

I have no empirical basis for forecasting the proportions of idle young men who would fall in the various categories I have described. Some will doubtlessly use the UBI as a way of continuing to be idle. But for others, the Doolittle Effect will be real.

Criminality

The third problematic category of people is chronic criminals. According to sociological theory that sees crime as a response to economic deprivation, the UBI should reduce crime. The UBI will provide a nice test of such theories. But the twentieth century provided a nice test, too, and the theories flunked. Poverty fell; crime rose.[56] The UBI may indirectly reduce crime through positive effects on family structure, but I will not forecast reduced crime as one of the UBI's positive effects. If it happens, it will be a bonus.

The Broadest Effect on the Underclass

These chapters are about immediate changes in tangible incentives, not about the longer-range effects. But I cannot leave the discussion of effects on the underclass without alluding to a broader effect of the UBI that may be the most important of all.

A powerful critique of the current system is that the people who make up the underclass have no reason to think they can be anything else. They are poorly educated, without job skills, and living in neighborhoods where prospects are bleak. The quest for dignity and self-respect takes the form of trying to beat the system, whether *the system* means the criminal code or the rules that surround the distribution of welfare. The more fortunate members of society may see such people as obstinately refusing to take advantage of the opportunities that exist. Seen from the perspective of the man who has never held a job or the woman who wants to have an infant to love, those opportunities look fraudulent.

The UBI does not exhort the young man to go out and get a job. It does not urge the young woman to delay childbearing. It does not do anything that tries to stage-manage their lives. The UBI provides a stake—prospectively for those under 21, in actuality for those who have turned 21. The UBI is not charity—everyone in the country turning 21 is getting the same thing. Ten thousand dollars of it is cash to be used as they wish, not little bundles of benefits to be allocated as the welfare bureaucracy sees fit. The UBI is deposited monthly into that most middle-class of institutions, a bank account. The UBI says to people who have never had reason to believe it before: "Your future is in your hands." And it is the truth.

7

Work Disincentives

The most serious practical objection to the UBI is its potential effect on work. For years, economists have found through quantitative analysis what common sense predicts: Make it easier not to work, and people work less. Unemployment insurance is the most obvious example, but almost any transfer payment linked to employment or wages has similar effects. Economists call them work disincentives.

Two specific populations who are responsive to work disincentives are discussed elsewhere: In the preceding chapter on the underclass, I discussed men who are out of the labor force under the current system. For this group, there is no downside to the UBI (the men in it are already out of the labor force) and some upside (the Doolittle Effect). The other population is women who now work but would quit to become full-time housewives, discussed in Chapter 10. For them, I argue that the reduction in work outside the home represents a positive net effect, not a negative one. This chapter restricts itself to the people who might stop working because of the cash grant, not to better themselves in some other way and not to devote more time to making a home, but to loaf.

The UBI does not even require such people to be sneaky. It says to 21-year-olds, "If half a dozen of you want to pool your grants, rent a cottage on an inexpensive beach, and surf for the rest of your lives, the American taxpayer will support you." The question is how many people are likely to respond to the grant in that way or, more broadly, how labor force participation and work effort might be expected to change.

The following discussion works through a variety of scenarios, but here is where it will come out:

- Most of those who remain out of the labor force will be the same people who are out of the labor force under the current system.

- Most of the reductions in work effort will involve fewer hours worked, not fewer people working.

- Most of the people who leave the labor force will be college graduates who take time off between graduation and a permanent job or graduate school.

- The net decrease in work effort will be acceptable.

The key features of the UBI that lead to these conclusions are two buffer zones: the income level at which the grant begins to be paid back through the surtax, and the age at which the grant begins. By the time people have crossed these buffer zones, most of them will have passed the point at which living off the UBI is an acceptable alternative.

Buffer #1: A High Payback Point

I have designed the UBI to lure people into working until they are making so much money that they can't afford to quit.

To understand the problem that my rules are designed to solve, consider the experience of the 1970s, when the US government conducted the negative income tax experiment in a few test cities (Chapter 1). The evaluators found that large numbers of low-income young people dropped out of the labor force. The reason was simple: When the government fills in income up to a floor, people in jobs that pay less than the floor are working for nothing.

The work disincentive does not stop there. Even a person making more than the floor can be working for pennies an hour. If the floor is $200 a week, for example, and the job offer is the minimum wage of $290 for a 40-hour week, taking the job means working for $2.25 an hour. For practical purposes, the choices for people near the NIT's income floor were to take the NIT and not work, work off the books and get the NIT illegally, or work on the books and be a chump. Many people decided not to be chumps, and it's hard to blame them.

Policy planners for the negative income tax experiment tinkered with the incentives so that a dollar of income did not produce a full dollar's reduction in the subsidy, but they were up against mathematical constraints. There is no way to set a simple floor under income anywhere near the poverty line that does not have disastrous consequences for work effort among people just getting into the labor market.

Setting the start of the payback of the grant at $30,000 is an Alexandrian solution, cutting the knot rather than trying to untie it. "Keep every cent you make until you reach $30,000, then we'll talk," it says. By that time, it is too late to back out. If a man is earning $30,000 a year under the UBI, still getting the full grant, he is taking home a gross income of $40,000. The 10 percent surtax on incremental income when he gets a raise to, say, $32,000 amounts to $200, leaving him with a cash gross of $41,800, compared with $10,000 if he stops working. The fact that someone starts paying a few hundred dollars in surtax when he first gets past $30,000 in earned income has no meaningful effect on his calculations about whether to continue working.

For someone making $45,000 per year, the tax on the grant has risen to $2,100. By that point there may be some effects on wage structure and on work effort at the margin. But the number of people making $45,000 who will decide to leave work altogether and exchange a $52,900 lifestyle (the sum of wages and the remaining $7,900 in cash from the grant) for a $10,000 lifestyle will be small.

Buffer #2: The Age at Which the Grant Begins

The second buffer zone is established by the three-year gap between the end of high school and the beginning of the grant. During that time, young people either need to earn their own living or continue to be supported by their parents. Consider how this buffer zone applies to specific groups of young people turning 21 and newly eligible for the grant.

People Who Go to Work After High School. As of 2014, 34 percent of all young people ages 18 to 20 were neither in high school nor in college.[57] Under the UBI, they would not yet be getting the grant, and getting a job after high school will make as much sense under the UBI as it does now.

Those who go to work will typically change jobs several times during the three years from 18 to 21, usually to take a better job requiring more skills for more money. The average 21-year-old who worked at least 48 weeks in 2014 made $24,085.[58] For that typical young worker looking at the first UBI check, the choice is to continue working and live on $34,085 a year, or stop working and live on $10,000 a year. The high school graduate who has been working has already reached the point where quitting usually carries an unacceptably high price tag. The same calculus applies generally. Suppose that a less fortunate 21-year-old is still making only $10,000. Under the UBI, he could quit and have the same income. But another way of looking at it, and a potent one for any 21-year-old who has unsatisfied consumer desires, is that he is about to get a $10,000 raise if he keeps doing what he is already doing.

These financial calculations are independent of another effect of the buffer zone: By the time they are 21, many high school graduates are not working just because of the money. They have acquired the habit of employment, are in skilled jobs that have good prospects, and are enjoying their work.

People Who Go to College. By the time they reach 21, those who went straight to college after high school are usually about three-quarters of the way through an undergraduate degree. The onset of the grant is irrelevant to their long-term plans. Most have career ambitions. All expect to get jobs paying a decent wage, and many of them reasonably expect to be making more than $60,000 (the point at which they are paying back the maximum 50 percent of the UBI) within a few years of graduation. The only effect of the UBI is short term, giving more students the options that are already enjoyed by large numbers of college students from affluent families—travel abroad and unpaid internships being the most common choices. I assume that the UBI will have this effect, encouraging a significant number of college students to take some time off either during college or after graduation. Should this effect of the UBI be considered bad or good? Good, in my view. (I encouraged my own children not to go directly to graduate school or begin a permanent career when they got their BA.) But I will not insist on this interpretation. An uncontroversial conclusion is that a few years off for this group will, at worst, do no great harm.

How many students will be permanently seduced into living in a beach house with their buddies, surfing their lives away? I could work through the pressures on them, social and economic, not to do so, but doing so seems like overkill. There's no reason to think that the number is going to be much larger than the number of college graduates in the 1960s who became permanent hippies. Playing is fun for a while, but it gets old quickly.

If the UBI were to be implemented, it is prudent to assume that some decrease in work effort would occur. But the two buffer zones offer protections against work disincentives that none of the previous plans for a negative income tax have incorporated. If the UBI were to become a live political possibility, then the arguments I have presented should be subjected to econometric modeling, and the range of likely outcomes should be calibrated as accurately as possible. But we are now at a much earlier stage, where the question is whether unacceptable work disincentives should keep us from considering the UBI any further. The answer to that question seems plainly to be *no*.

Going to College: The UBI Versus the Current System for Low-Income Students

Among the programs axed under the UBI are all government-paid student loans and scholarships. In their place, the UBI gives every young person cash. The amount of cash compares favorably with the federal scholarship program. As of 2015, federal Pell Grants top out at $5,775 per year.[59] The UBI compares favorably with student loans insofar as no repayment is required. But the grant does not begin until the 21st birthday. The UBI forces some students from low-income families to wait.

It is not clear how many would need to wait. Under the UBI, low-income students could use the guarantee of the UBI as collateral to take to banks and to college financial offices. It is also plausible that private foundations will increase their scholarship programs for low-income students when the federal government gets out of the scholarship business. But I nonetheless stipulate that some low-income students who now go directly to college after high school will, under the UBI, need to wait until they are 21. Is this good or bad? As in the case of taking time off after college, parents will differ in their opinions for reasons that are hard to evaluate empirically. I am in favor of encouraging students to wait. Ask someone who teaches in a public university where many students enter after some years working or serving in the military, and I predict you will hear that the seriousness with which these students approach their education contrasts favorably with that of the students who come to college directly from high school. But once again I do not insist on my interpretation. Under the UBI, every young person—*every* young person, not just those who obtain scholarships and grants under the current system—will have the financial wherewithal to further their education. They just won't have it until age 21.

PART III

The Larger Purpose

8

The Pursuit of Happiness in Advanced Societies

Put aside the immediate effects of the UBI and consider instead a completely different proposition: *The real problem for most people in advanced societies has nothing to do with the historic ills of poverty and injustice. Those are on the road to being solved. For most people today, the problem is how to live meaningful lives in an age of plenty and security. The UBI will help in solving that problem.*

In this chapter, I lay out my framework for thinking about the proposition. The subsequent three chapters discuss how the UBI can revitalize three domains of civil society that are crucial to the pursuit of happiness: work, family, and community.

The Problem

Throughout history, much of the meaning of life was linked to the challenge of staying alive. Staying alive required being a contributing part of a community. Staying alive required forming a family and having children to care for you in your old age. The knowledge that sudden death could happen any time required attention to spiritual issues.

Life in an age of plenty and security requires none of those things. Being part of a community is not necessary. Marriage is not necessary. Children are not necessary. Attention to spiritual issues is not necessary. It is not only possible but easy to go through life with a few friends and serial sex partners, earning a good living, having a good time, and dying in old age with no reason to think that one has done anything more significant than while away the time.

Perhaps, as the song says, that's all there is. But if you disagree and think that to live a human life has—or can have—transcendental meaning, join me on an exploration that will take us far afield from annuity values and health insurance pools, but will ultimately, I believe, point to the truly momentous effect of the UBI: the revitalization of the institutions through which people live satisfying lives.

Western Europe as the Canary in the Coal Mine

"An age of plenty and security" refers most accurately to Western Europe. Western Europe adopted the welfare state earlier than the United States and implemented it more completely. It was implemented earliest and most sweepingly in Germany, France, the Low Countries, and Scandinavia. Putting aside for a moment the budgetary crises looming for these countries in the years ahead, they succeeded in their central goals. On almost any dimension of material well-being, these countries lead the world. Their indices of economic equality are the highest, and their indices of economic deprivation are the lowest. In the minds of many, the European welfare state represents the ideal America should emulate.[60]

It is an ideal only for a particular way of looking at life. It accepts that the purpose of life is to while away the time as pleasantly as possible, and the purpose of government is to enable people to do so with as little effort as possible—what I will call the Europe Syndrome.

Europe's short workweeks and frequent vacations are one symptom of the syndrome. The idea of work as a means to self-fulfillment has faded. The view of work as a necessary evil, interfering with the higher good of leisure, dominates. The Europe Syndrome also consists of ways in which vocation is impeded. Job security is high, but so is the danger that if you leave a job to seek a better one, you won't be able to find one. Starting a new business is agonizingly difficult. Elaborate restrictions impede employers from rewarding merit and firing the incompetent. The Europe Syndrome is dismissive of all the ways in which work can become a vocation and a vocation can become a central source of satisfaction in life.

The precipitous decline of marriage is another symptom. The marriage rate has dropped in the United States, but it is still about 50 percent higher than in the advanced welfare states of Western Europe.[61] Fertility rates in most European countries are far below replacement.[62] The incidence of deliberate childlessness—choosing to have no children at all—is rising.[63] The choice among women to have a child without a father present is rising.[64]

These are phenomena of modernity that are shared to some degree by many types of societies, but the advanced welfare state facilitates a particular mindset toward them. It removes many of the traditional economic incentives to marry. It treats children as a burden to their parents that must be lightened through child allowances, subsidies, and services. It objectifies the trade-offs: Children are no longer the central expression of a marriage and a life, but an option to be compared with other options. Have a baby or buy a vacation home? Have a baby or preserve one's leisure time? Why have a child, when children are so expensive, so much trouble—and, after all, what good are they, really? The advanced welfare state facilitates a culture of self-absorption—absorption not in some great ambition, but in the whiling away of life as pleasantly as possible.

The secularization of Europe is another symptom of the Europe Syndrome. Western European churches are nearly empty. Europeans have broadly come to believe that humans are a collection of activated chemicals that, after a period of time, deactivate—nothing more. The causal arrow linking the welfare state and secularization could operate in either of two ways. If one believes there is no God and no transcendent meaning to life, then one might see the disappearance of religion as a good thing. Religion is just a way to cope with anxiety and misery. Take away the anxiety and misery, and religion falls away, too. Conversely, one may start by believing that God exists and life has transcendent meaning, but that the welfare state distracts humans from thinking about such things. Give people plenty and security, and they will fall into spiritual torpor. Whichever logic one employs, the degree of secularization within Europe is unique—no culture in recorded history has been nearly as secular as contemporary Europe's.

The same absorption in whiling away life as pleasantly as possible explains why Western Europe has become a continent without dreams of greatness nor the means to reacquire greatness. Europe's former scientific preeminence has vanished, as young scientists flock to American universities and corporations, even when they would prefer to live in their homelands, because they cannot hope for the professional freedom or financial support to pursue their work until they have crept up the bureaucratic chain. Even Europe's popular culture is largely borrowed from America, and its high culture can draw only on its glorious past—it has no contemporary high culture worthy of the name. All of Europe combined has neither the military force nor the political will to defend itself. The only thing Europe has left is economic size, and even that is growing at a slower pace than elsewhere. When life becomes an extended picnic, with nothing of importance to do, ideas of greatness become an irritant.

Such is the nature of the Europe Syndrome. The next issue is whether it is so awful. What's wrong with a society in which everyone can while away life as pleasantly as possible? The answer requires an inquiry into the difference between pleasure and happiness.

Happiness Taken Seriously

A familiar word used in its original meaning can sometimes provoke fresh thinking. *Happiness* is one of those words. Social scientists may talk about quality of life, utility functions, and cost-effectiveness, but the ultimate measure of the success of a policy is that it enables people to pursue happiness in the sense that Jefferson used happiness in the Declaration of Independence. His understanding drew from a tradition going back to Aristotle, but its gist can be stated quickly and simply: *Happiness is lasting and justified satisfaction with one's life as a whole.* If that is indeed the nature of happiness, it cannot be synonymous with pleasure. Consider the key words in that definition: *lasting* and *justified*.

Lasting says that when you think about how happy you are, you don't base it on momentary gratification. A bowl of hot buttered popcorn provides a satisfaction of a sort, as does a good movie, but they are not lasting satisfactions. The constraint of *lasting* limits the qualifying satisfactions to a narrow set.

Justified implies that satisfactions are not equally valid. Specifically, *justified* draws from an idea about happiness that the ancients and the founders alike took for granted: Happiness is inextricably linked with the exercise of one's abilities and the practice of virtue. Happiness consists of something more than feeling good. A pig cannot be happy. A person permanently high on drugs cannot be happy. An idle person cannot be happy. A selfish or cruel person cannot be happy. None meet the *justified* criterion.

Some Propositions About the Raw Materials for Happiness. If you consider yourself happy, ask yourself about the sources of your happiness. To the extent that you are not happy, what is lacking? I will suggest some answers, and you may judge how closely they fit your own.

Think of the pursuit of happiness as a process that each of us conducts by employing five raw materials. Two of these raw materials are passive: enough material resources and enough safety. This is as simple as saying that you cannot be happy if you are starving or constantly in danger.[65] I call them *passive* raw materials because possessing enough material resources and safety does not in itself make us happy, but their absence can keep us from being happy. Public policy directly affects the passive ingredients for the pursuit of happiness. Providing enough safety is the function of the police, the courts, and the armed forces. Providing enough material resources was historically the indirect effect of a government's sound economic policy and, more recently, has been adopted as the job of the welfare state.

I propose that the three *active* raw materials for the pursuit of happiness— those things which themselves can engender a sense of happiness—are intimate relationships with other human beings, vocation, and self-respect. A few words about each:

Intimate relationships with other human beings are achieved most commonly through a spouse and children, but they can also occur with friends, mentors, protégés, or colleagues. Conversely, unhappiness commonly results from the absence of satisfying, deep personal relationships.

Vocation might mean a job, or it might mean some other activity that engages one's passion. The chief characteristic of vocation as I am using the word is that it represents something a person is good at, his way of expressing his skills, of achieving his potential. Conversely, lack of happiness is likely to have something to do with a sense that one has never found such an outlet— that one has no vocation. *Vocation* as I am using the word could also be defined as self-fulfillment.

Self-respect is to some degree a necessary condition for happiness. It is hard to imagine a person being happy who does not have self-respect. But it can also serve as a substitute for the other raw materials. Perhaps a person has no vocation. Perhaps he does not have children, a good marriage, or deep friendships, but at least he can carry his head high in the world. Why he feels entitled to carry his head high depends on his ethical priorities. The reason might have to do with putting more into the world than he takes out, taking responsibility for people who depend on him, or following the dictates of his faith. One way or another, it is a matter of meeting standards of conduct that he values. Social philosopher Michael Walzer put it memorably when he contrasted self-esteem with self-respect. We can feel self-esteem if enough other people tell us flattering things about ourselves, Walzer observed, but others cannot convince us that we have self-respect: "Now conscience is the court, and conscience is a shared knowledge, an internalized acceptance of community standards. . . . [W]e can't ignore the standards, and we can't juggle the verdict. We do measure up, or we don't."[66]

Intimate relationships with other humans, a satisfying vocation, and self-respect: These, I propose, are the active ingredients for achieving lasting and justified satisfaction with life as a whole.[67] The obvious next question would seem to be how society can best supply those active ingredients—not just to a lucky few who are especially talented and self-reliant, but to everyone. But before we can tackle that question, we need to ask a more fundamental one. How does human nature play into both the pursuit of happiness and the construction of social institutions?

The Nature of Man as a Social Being

Whenever people propose policies and predict their effects, they are making assumptions about human nature. I make certain assumptions when I argue that the UBI will work. These assumptions about human nature are seldom stated explicitly, because often they bear no relationship to real human beings in real social groups. Consider the slogan "From each according to his ability, to each according to his needs" that inspired generations of socialists. The slogan sounds wonderful, but even socialists knew that real human beings in large numbers wouldn't behave that way. Thus it is no accident that socialist theory held that the right social and economic institutions would change human nature. Socialism not only promised a "new man," it *required* a new man.

I contend that the UBI would work because it is congruent with human nature as it actually exists. These are the three key characteristics of human nature I have in mind:

- Humans tend to act in ways that advance their own interests.

- Humans tend to have a desire for approbation from other human beings.

- Humans tend to take on responsibilities to the extent that circumstances require them to do so.

I use the word *tend* in all three instances. Exceptions exist, but the tendencies are so pronounced and so widespread that if you are trying to predict the outcomes from complex policy changes, you may reliably expect that these characteristics of human beings will be at work. A few words of elaboration about each:

Humans tend to act in ways that advance their own interests. This is about as basic as truths about human behavior come, but it should not be confused with the false idea that human beings consistently try to maximize their interests. People more commonly "satisfice," to use Herbert Simon's word, contenting themselves with less than the last drop that they could have squeezed out of their situation.[68] Humans also do not act exclusively in their own self-interest. Altruism is everywhere. Human beings reliably pursue self-interest and reliably respond to incentives, but with moderation—that's the sense of my proposition.

Humans tend to be social creatures, having an innate desire for approbation from other human beings. Philosophers have argued for centuries about whether man has an innate moral sense.[69] But Adam Smith made a more limited argument that enables us to sidestep the most difficult questions about the moral sense. In *The Theory of Moral Sentiments*, Smith invokes the image of a man raised alone on a desert island without any communication with another human being. Such a man could not possibly think of his own character, Smith pointed out, any more than he could think of his face as being handsome. He would lack any frame of reference. But put him together with other human beings and he cannot avoid having a frame of reference for considering his own character, just as he cannot avoid having a frame of reference for assessing whether he is handsome. Smith's subsequent argument comes down to the proposition that man was formed for society by an "original desire to please, and an original aversion to offend," feeling pleasure from approbation for its own sake and pain from disapprobation. These reinforcements may be in the form of fame and fortune, in the good opinion of coworkers or neighbors, in the praise of one's boss, or in the admiration of one's children.[70]

The desire for approbation is a de facto moral sense. Communities function better when people exhibit cooperativeness; behaviors that are cooperative tend to receive approbation; we behave cooperatively to get approbation. John Adams nearly paraphrased Smith, writing in 1790 that "as Nature intended men for society, she has endowed them with passions, appetites and propensities calculated . . . to render them useful to each other in their social connections." Of these passions, appetites, and propensities, Adams continued, none was more essential and remarkable than the desire of every man "to be observed, considered, esteemed, praised, beloved, and admired by his fellows."[71] To a twenty-first-century reader, there is nothing strange in the thought, even if there may be in the wording. It seems to be an empirical fact. People like to be thought well of, and this can be a powerful force for making civil society work without compulsion.

Humans tend to take on responsibilities to the extent that circumstances require them to do so. This proposition applies to behaviors small and large. If someone else will wash the dishes, we tend to let them; if someone else will feed the hungry, we tend to let them; if someone else will defend the nation, we tend to let them. But when we are told, "If you don't do it, no one else will," we also tend to respond. If you think this is too optimistic a view of human behavior, test it against your own life. Try to think of something that matters to you that will not get done if you don't do it and that you nonetheless will take no steps to do. You will have a hard time coming up with an example. If it is really true that you want the thing to be done, you are in a position to do it, and no one else will, you are extremely likely to do it.

I specified "really true" in that claim because there are all sorts of things that we would like to see done but to which we can contribute only symbolically. Feeding the hungry is a good example. The probability that I will take action if I learn that one of my neighbors needs food is 100 percent. The probability that I will support a soup kitchen in my community is 100 percent if my church runs it; still high if it is a soup kitchen run by people in my community; and small if we are talking about a consortium of soup kitchens serving the Middle Atlantic states. The probability that I will voluntarily contribute extra taxes to the federal government's Supplemental Nutrition Assistance Program program is zero. Our willingness to assume responsibilities is intimately linked to the effect that we as individuals believe we can have.

Linking Up the Raw Materials with Human Nature

Taking together the raw materials for the pursuit of happiness and the nature of the human as a social being, I propose that there are just four domains within which humans achieve lasting and justified satisfaction with life as a whole: work, family, community, and faith. Over the course of almost 30 years of making that claim, I have asked countless audiences to give me a fifth one that is independent of the first four. No one ever has been able to nominate a persuasive candidate (with the caveat that *work* doesn't have to be paid employment).

So let's assume that those four domains—the "institutions of meaning," as Arthur Brooks has evocatively labeled them—are our only options.[72] For one of them, faith, the UBI is probably irrelevant. I can imagine some indirect positive effects, but they are only possibilities. The great religious faiths have not flourished because of the things that the UBI facilitates. But the UBI's interactions with work, family, and community are many and, in my judgment, are likely to have profound consequences. The UBI has the potential to revive and enrich America's historic civil society. The next three chapters describe why.

9

Work

A central satisfaction of life comes from the sense of doing something one values and doing it well. Being engaged in that activity regularly means that one has a vocation. A few people know early in their lives that they are called to a vocation. More commonly, people come to a vocation by trial and error—by working at many jobs.

For many people, work never becomes a vocation. Sometimes these people find a surrogate elsewhere, through an avocation or involvement in the community. The UBI can help generate these sources of satisfaction as well, as described in Chapter 11. But the topic of this chapter is vocation through working. The role the UBI plays is twofold. The UBI makes it easier to find a vocation by changing jobs and easier for a person to accumulate the capital to pursue a dream.

Changing Jobs

Few teenagers finish high school already knowing what job will make them happy. Or they may think they know, but change their minds. This is as true of those who go to college as those who do not—that's why students change their majors so often. The process of finding a job that makes one happy often continues well into a person's twenties, if not beyond. Only for a lucky few does it mean finding the perfect job. Some people find that working outdoors makes otherwise mundane jobs attractive. For others, working at home has the same effect. Jobs vary along many dimensions, and the history of most people who find satisfaction in a job is one of incrementally improving their situation over a period of years. This typically has meant changing employers and moving geographically.

Europe is especially useful as the canary in this part of the coal mine. Government regulation has made the costs of hiring an employee so high, and made it so hard to dismiss an employee, that the European labor market has become rigid. New jobs are scarce, and long-term unemployment is high. So an employee who has a job he hates nonetheless will tend to keep it rather than quit and look for a better one. European peasants used to be tied to the land. In this new version of serfdom, European workers are tied to their jobs.

A major strength of the American economy is its history of high labor mobility. As in other aspects of the welfare state, however, the United States is on the European track. The UBI does nothing about one of the main sources of increasing immobility—the regulatory mandates that increasingly constrain hiring and firing—but it does promote freedom to move from job to job.

The main effect follows from the widespread reductions the UBI will produce in job-related medical coverage and retirement plans. Consider the situation facing a low- or middle-income worker who is not happy in his job under the current system. He might be willing to go without a salary for a few months, but giving up untaxed health insurance benefits and paying for health insurance out of pocket may make the price of leaving too high, even with the Affordable Care Act. If he also has to give up retirement benefits that are not yet vested, the price can be prohibitively high. Under the UBI, millions more people will have portable retirement accounts and medical insurance. By the same token, the freedom of millions more people to look for a better job will be increased, and this is an essential part of incrementally finding a vocation.

The same effect will be felt by people who are out of the labor market altogether. Consider a single mother who has successfully gotten TANF, housing assistance, Medicaid, and food stamps in a city where the job market is bad. For her to pull up stakes and move to a city where the job market is better is foolish. If she doesn't find a job, she will have to go through the whole uncertain and stressful application process again and survive all its delays before she begins to get renewed support. Under the UBI, she faces none of those costs. Government no longer ties her to a place.

Pursuing a Dream

When introducing the UBI, I acknowledged that it could be implemented with requirements for contributions to retirement, but said that I thought it would be better without that requirement. We have come to one reason why: The UBI gives people a way of accumulating enough money to try to realize their ambitions: to go to college after all, even though they've got a family to support; to start their own business; or to leave Dubuque and move to Alaska. The dreams can take numberless variations, but people working in low-income jobs and responsible for families usually have to abandon them. The UBI does not make such dreams easy to realize, but it does bring them into the realm of the possible, given discipline and hard work.

That last proviso—"given discipline and hard work"—points to one of the ways in which the UBI is likely to have positive side effects. The UBI does not provide enough money in any one year to finance much of anything. However, it does provide enough money so that someone can save over the course of three or four years, then go to the bank and say, "Here is what I have done, planning for this day, and how much I have accumulated," and thereby have a chance of getting a loan. That prospect, and the experience of saving over those years, are themselves valuable outcomes. The UBI will expand that prospect to millions of people who have never considered it before. Within those millions, some subset will acquire habits of self-discipline and long-term planning that will positively affect their lives on many dimensions. And, not incidentally, many within that subset will succeed in achieving their original dream.

That leads to the question of those who try and fail. They save for four years, get a loan, start that cherished new business—and it fails. Has the UBI's effect been good or bad? Reasonable people will disagree. My position is that failure is a positive part of life. The cliché about learning more from our failures than our successes is true. The cliché that some of the best things in our lives come about because of failure is true. The cliché that life is not a destination but a journey is true. If the UBI enables millions of people to pursue their dreams who would not have been able to pursue them otherwise, I count that as a success in itself. And for those who have failed, the UBI continues to provide a backstop. They have lost the money that went into their venture, but they still have the grant, plus whatever they can make from a job, to pick themselves back up again.

Others will disagree, valuing security more than I do. There is no disputing tastes, but this thought is relevant: If you are a person who values security above all else, the UBI gives you the option of being as conservative as you wish: putting all of your retirement money into bonds instead of stocks; or paying for a health care plan that leaves no chance whatsoever that you will be left uncovered for anything. But why dictate that everyone must behave as you do? Why not let people decide for themselves how they want to live their lives? If they make mistakes, they will have been their mistakes, not yours. Those who want to impose security on others have no idea whether they are doing the right thing for someone else's ultimate happiness. They shouldn't have the right to do so.

The opportunity to try different paths is at the heart of acquiring a vocation. It is one of the greatest advantages that youths from economically secure families enjoy. The UBI goes a long way toward extending that opportunity to everyone.

10

Family

The UBI will affect the functioning of all kinds of families. I covered some of those effects in the discussion of the underclass in Chapter 6—effects on cohabitating partners, single mothers, and the ability of parents and siblings to bring pressure to bear on adult members of the family who are dysfunctional.

The broadest of all effects on the functioning of families will be the simple infusion of resources into low-income families. Consider a low-income couple in their fifties with two adult children. Those four people, tied by the bonds of family, have an aggregate of $40,000 more per year than they have under the current system. That can make a big difference in their ability to help each other in times of trouble, to celebrate good times, or to do such basic things as see each other more often if they live in different cities. This will be true of all kinds of low-income families, whether headed by a single parent or by partners who are married or cohabiting, gay or straight. For that matter, it will affect childless couples. A low-income family consisting just of two partners will have $20,000 more than they would have without the UBI, and there are many ways in which those resources can benefit their family life.

My focus in this chapter, however, is the traditional definition of family—a married couple with children—and three types of effects on the formation and functioning of traditional families: effects on the decision to marry, effects on people after they are married, and effects that make the traditional family more autonomous and responsible.

Effects on the Decision to Marry

One effect of the UBI will be to make marriage economically easier for low-income people. If this effect were to play out uniformly across different types of people, it would produce good marriages and bad in proportions that are hard to forecast in advance. But it will not play out uniformly. The UBI's greatest effect will be on those couples who worry about money before deciding to get married, and its smallest effect will be on those who get married on a whim. Or, to put it another way, the UBI will have the most effect on the most responsible young people and the least effect on the least responsible, producing a strong bias toward enabling good marriages to occur.[73]

But just because the UBI makes marriage easier does not necessarily mean that large numbers of people will choose to marry who do not marry now. So let us consider more specifically how the UBI affects the choice to marry, cohabit, live separately, or end a relationship.

In trying to think through how the changed incentives will play out, much depends on the answer to one question: How much difference does marriage make to a father's legal rights and obligations toward the child he fathers?

When Marriage Is Everything. At the one extreme is a marriage-is-everything regime in which the biological father of a child has neither rights and nor obligations regarding his child unless he marries—close to the de facto framework for marriage that applied in the United States and Europe until the 1960s.[74] Under a marriage-is-everything regime in the presence of the UBI, the woman knows she must marry to have any claim on the father of her children. She also knows that even an unemployed boyfriend has $10,000 in income. If she becomes pregnant, this provides her with a strong incentive to marry. That same $10,000 gives a reluctant boyfriend an extra incentive to avoid marriage. Those are the same competing incentives that used to apply in the United States when the legal regime was effectively marriage-is-everything and the welfare state was still small. The result in that era was that women actively avoided becoming pregnant without the assurance of marriage, and the percentage of children born out of wedlock was in the low single digits. Comparable dynamics are fostered by the UBI under a marriage-is-everything regime. If the nation were to move toward restoring the unique obligations associated with marriage, the UBI would provide a powerful incentive for a woman to require marriage before bearing a man's child. It is hard to think of any other single change that would have as many positive effects on the next generation of children.[75]

When Marriage Doesn't Count. At the other extreme is a marriage-doesn't-count regime in which the standing of the unmarried biological father is identical to the standing of the married biological father.

If marriage doesn't count, the UBI has no effect on the decision to marry. It adds money to the income of both of the partners, but it does not change the economic incentives to marry. If marriage doesn't matter legally, the decision to marry is based exclusively on noneconomic considerations.

The reality is that the nation has been moving toward a marriage-doesn't-count regime for decades, which I consider to be a mistake, but it is hard to see how the UBI will makes matters worse. Cohabitation will continue to spread, but the UBI doesn't make marriage less desirable.[76]

Effects on Marriage Among the Married

Whatever happens to the laws surrounding marriage, large numbers of people will continue to get married. The effects of the UBI on existing marriages are limited to families for whom the cash grant is an important part of total family income. Those effects are of four kinds: effects on divorce, effects that make it easier for mothers to have both children and a career, effects that make it easier for mothers to stay at home, and effects that increase the autonomy and responsibility of the family as a unit.

Why "Mothers" Instead of "Fathers"?

Yes, I know: Sometimes it's the woman who wants to work and the man who wants to raise the children. Such couples remain comparatively rare. I judge that to refer to "mothers" conveys the reality of what would happen under the UBI more accurately than the politically correct "partners."

Effects on Divorce. Under the current system, women who forgo careers to be full-time housewives and mothers are vulnerable to being forced into the labor market in midlife without job skills or experience. For affluent couples, this vulnerability is counterbalanced by adequate alimony and child support. The UBI provides a similar counterbalance for women in low-income and middle-income households. One may be opposed to divorce and yet in favor of measures that free women from the economic compulsion to remain in a bad marriage. On the other side of the ledger, the UBI's financial guarantee will make it easier for salvageable marriages to break up. I know of no way to forecast what the mix will be.

Effects on Mothers Who Work Outside the Home. As I tackle the delicate topic of whether mothers stay at home or have a job outside the home, the crucial distinction is between mothers who work because they like their jobs and those who work out of economic necessity.

Mothers who prefer to work outside the home. As matters stand now, affluence makes a crucial difference for women who want to work outside the home. They have the money to hire nannies or send their children to good day care centers. The UBI makes it easier for mothers in low-income and middle-income households to do the same thing. For families in which the woman is already working, the UBI will ease the financial strain of paying for child care. For families in which the woman is not working but wants to, the UBI will enable her to do so by providing resources for buying child care. I interpret both effects as being good for the marriages in question.[77] The UBI does nothing to persuade mothers with children to work outside the home. It makes it easier for them to do so if they want to.

Mothers who work out of economic necessity. Now the issue is the mother who is working but, given the option, would rather work fewer hours or none at all so she can spend more times as homemaker and mother. Once again, the UBI is not going to affect the decisions of women in affluent households for whom the grant is a negligible percentage of the family's income. But the UBI is likely to have large effects on households with incomes well into the middle class.

To see why the importance of the UBI reaches so far up the income ladder, remember that a woman who does not work gets the cash grant no matter how much her husband makes. For many women with young children who work only because they have to help make ends meet, the grant can easily represent the difference between financial hardship and being able to get along on the husband's income.

Consider a household in which the husband makes $60,000 and the wife makes $30,000, adding up to a solidly middle-class family income of $90,000. When a child is born, financial obligations are likely to be in place that make it difficult to get along without a second income. So under the current system, the wife continues to work, except that now she must pay (let's say) $7,000 a year for day care, and the family gets along on an income of $83,000. The UBI makes it easier to tweak the family finances so that the wife can quit her job if she wishes. In this specific instance, the family may not find it feasible under the current system to go from a family income of $83,000 to $60,000, but the day after the UBI is passed they realize they could manage on their new net income of $76,500 they would have if the wife quits work altogether.[78]

For scenarios in which the combined income from the two wage-earners is smaller, these effects of the UBI get larger. Insofar as the UBI permits more women to do what they prefer to do regarding a central life role—mother—it is unambiguously positive for those women and positive for the children as well.

More families in which one person is staying at home full time out of choice will also be good for marriage. A marriage can be filled with family activities, or it can be stripped down. The more time that is filled by careers, the more stripping-down of family life has to occur. It is not a matter of choice. Weekends are a different kind of experience in a family where all the domestic chores of the week must be crowded into Saturday and Sunday versus one where they are not. The availability for volunteer work at the local school differs between those two households. The availability to be a neighbor in times of need differs. The availability to care for aging parents differs. The availability to be a Sunday school teacher differs. All of these activities on the part of either parent are in addition to the childrearing activities that can fill a marriage or be stripped down. It is a simple relationship: The more resources that are devoted to a marriage, the richer that marriage is likely to be. The richer the marriages in a community, the more the community thrives. The UBI's effect on enabling wives to stay home if they wish could be one of its most important ones.

Effects That Make the Family More Autonomous and Responsible

The UBI returns core functions and responsibilities to the family, and doing so is likely to have a revitalizing effect on the institution as a whole.

Consider this paradox: Taking on a wife and then becoming a father is what a young man, full of wild oats, should least like to do. And yet throughout history and across cultures, young men have yearned to marry. In some cultures, they have scrimped and saved to accumulate bride prices. In our own culture until well into the twentieth century, young men consciously behaved in ways that demonstrated they would be good providers so that they could convince a woman to marry them. Why have young men so consistently acted against what their hormones would lead them to do in a state of nature?

The direct answer is that marriage used to be the only way that most men could get regular sexual access to a woman—a powerful incentive. But that only pushes the question back further. Why should women have so consistently withheld sexual access until marriage? Again there is a direct answer: The woman was left holding the baby. Before the advent of the welfare state, women could not afford the risk of sex without a commitment from the man.

If that were the full explanation of why young men yearned to marry, the UBI wouldn't make any difference. Nothing is going to repeal the sexual revolution, and the UBI provides a woman with the resources to raise a child on her own if necessary. But the bald biological and economic incentives I just described are only part of the explanation. Over the eons required for us to become *Homo sapiens*, humans living in demanding environments had a survival advantage if the man stuck around after they mated, suggesting that by this time a male's genetic makeup contains predispositions not only to sow wild oats, but also to be a family man. Whether he ever becomes a family man depends on how culture mediates these competing impulses.

Historically, culture has taken the incentives I just described and pieced together a narrative around them consisting of norms, rewards, and punishments. In the case of young males, most cultures provided for a period of sowing wild oats but also said to them that the way to enter the fraternity of men was by becoming a husband and father. That message was based on a truth: the welfare of the community depended upon the formation of stable families. Being a husband and father became the badge of being an adult male because those roles were laden with responsibilities and obligations.

Now consider the phrase that is so often applied to social welfare systems: the safety net. It is wonderfully apt. People who know that a net is below them do reckless things that they wouldn't do otherwise. Under the current system, the net is there regardless of how people behave. Under the UBI, people have ample raw materials for a net, but they must weave it for themselves. People have to make choices, and it is possible to make the wrong choices. The potential rewards from marriage increase for low-income men and women because under the UBI the economic assets they bring to the marriage jump by $10,000 each. Those assets, combined and used prudently, give them the prospect of a bright and secure future. Similarly, the potential risks increase: Men and women alike have more to lose economically if their prospective spouses are irresponsible. I do not mean to sound naïve. People have made bad marriage choices throughout history and will continue to do so under any regime. But the UBI restores some of the traditional narrative that in the past led people to look beyond short-term sexual attraction and think about long-term effects.

Under the UBI, everyone still has the option of remaining single, moving in and out of relationships. But most people want something deeper and more lasting than that, something that looks like marriage traditionally defined. Under the UBI, marriage once again becomes the locus within which a man and woman can make a future together, laden with responsibilities and obligations that cannot be put aside.

I have provided a number of scenarios without any way to estimate which ones are the most likely. My own conclusion is based on a few core propositions that fall from the discussion in Chapter 8, applied here to marriage:

- The yearning for a lasting, intimate sexual relationship is hardwired into both women and men. Sexual proclivities among men and women differ in many ways, but both sexes want a mate.

- The current decline in marriage is not a function of modernity, but of the welfare state. The welfare state systematically competes with the natural attraction to marriage.[79]

- To restore the vitality of marriage, it is not necessary that policy do anything to encourage marriage. Policy simply needs to stop getting in the way.

- The UBI stops policy from getting in the way.

If these propositions are not correct, the UBI leaves marriage no worse off than it is now. If they are correct, the UBI will give marriage renewed meaning and vitality.

11

Community

The effects of the UBI on America's civic culture are potentially transforming and, in my view, are likely to constitute the most important single contribution of the UBI.

As government's role spread during the last 70 years, it has crowded out America's most effective resource for dealing with human needs. The UBI returns the stuff of life to the hands of civil society, and civil society is where American exceptionalism was grounded. Here is Alexis de Tocqueville, writing in the 1830s, on the American genius for voluntary association:

> Americans of all ages, all stations in life, and all types of dispositions are forever forming associations. There are not only commercial and industrial associations in which all take part, but others of a thousand different types—religious, moral, serious, futile, very general and very limited, immensely large and very minute. Americans combine to give fêtes, found seminaries, build churches, distribute books, and send missionaries to the antipodes. Hospitals, prisons, and schools take place in that way. Finally, if they want to proclaim a truth or propagate some feeling by the encouragement of a great example, they form an association. In every case, at the head of any new undertaking, where in France you would find the government or in England some territorial magnate, in the United States you are sure to find an association.[80]

The tradition continues today, evident in private philanthropic endeavors that are much rarer in Europe, and in the continuing social and religious organizations that are still an important part of life in working-class and middle-class America. But much has changed as well, for reasons that Tocqueville anticipated:

> A government could take the place of some of the largest associations in America, and some particular states of the Union have already attempted that. But what political power could ever carry on the vast multitude of lesser undertakings which associations daily enable American citizens to control? . . . The more government takes the place of associations, the more will individuals lose the idea of forming associations and need the government to come to their help. That is a vicious circle of cause and effect.[81]

The simple number of associations continues to increase to this day. But the newcomers are no longer associations that take on social tasks for themselves. Rather, they are advocacy groups that seek to influence how the government will do those tasks. The experience of voluntary associations based on broad memberships that actually performed the social tasks vindicated Tocqueville's prediction. They were still growing into the 1920s. Then their membership declined precipitously.[82]

This is not the place to untangle all the ways in which changes in American society affected voluntary associations, but two large events are among them. First came the Social Security Act of 1935, which created both Social Security and Aid to Families with Dependent Children. Each program took what had been a major arena of private activity into the federal government. Thirty years later came Lyndon Johnson's Great Society and the proliferation of social programs that accompanied it, proclaiming in effect that there was no longer any aspect of poverty and deprivation that the federal government would not take the lead in solving.

The Civic Culture We Have Nearly Lost

To convey what has been lost, it is necessary to tell the story of how extensive civic participation used to be. It begins with the network of fraternal associations for dealing with misfortune or old age through mutual insurance, such as the Odd Fellows, Elks, Masons, Moose, Redmen, and Knights of Pythias. Some were organized around specific occupations. Some were linked to membership in an ethnic group: Hebrew, Irish, or Italian. Most of the associations run by whites excluded blacks in those years, but that did not keep blacks from developing their own fraternal associations.[83]

Few people today realize the size and reach of these networks. In the mid-1920s, the National Fraternal Congress had 120,000 lodges.[84] The Odd Fellows had about 16 million members and the Knights of Pythias about 6 million.[85] So extensive were the fraternal organizations that an official of the New Hampshire Bureau of Labor could write in 1894 that "the tendency to join fraternal organizations for the purpose of obtaining care and relief in the event of sickness and insurance for the family in case of death is well-nigh universal."[86] Today, the remnants of these fraternal organizations perform shadows of their former functions.

Besides their mutual insurance functions, the fraternal organizations supported extensive social service activities. In that task they were supplemented by a long list of other charities exclusively focused on assistance to nonmembers. It is difficult to convey the magnitude of the effort to help the poor prior to the advent of the welfare state because that effort was so decentralized, but consider just a few statistics from New York City at the turn of the twentieth century. Here is the roster of activities discovered in a survey of 112 Protestant churches in Manhattan and the Bronx: 48 industrial schools, 45 libraries or reading rooms, 44 sewing schools, 40 kindergartens, 29 small sum savings banks and loan associations, 21 employment offices, 20 gymnasia and swimming pools, eight medical dispensaries, seven full-day nurseries, and four lodging houses.[87]

Those are just some of the Protestant churches in two boroughs of New York City, and it is not a complete list of the activities shown in the report. Now suppose I could add (I do not have the data) the activities in the other boroughs. Then add the activities of the rest of the Protestant churches. Then add the activities of the New York Catholic diocese. Then add those of the Jewish charities. After all that, suppose I could tally the activities of a completely separate and extensive web of secular voluntary associations. Perhaps the numbers from a very different setting will indicate how long that list might have been: When one small Midwestern state, Iowa, mounted a food conservation program in World War I, it engaged the participation of 2,873 church congregations and 9,630 chapters of 31 different secular fraternal associations.[88]

In evaluating such evidence, two issues must be separated. If the question is whether the philanthropic network successfully dealt with all the human needs that existed, the answer is obviously no. Dire poverty existed in the presence of all this activity. But that's not the right question. The assistance was being given in the context of national wealth that in 1900 amounted to a per capita gross domestic product (GDP) of about $6,808 in today's dollars, less than one-sixth of per capita GDP in 2014.[89] About two-thirds of the nation's nonfarm families were below the poverty line as presently defined.[90] I must put it as an assertion because the aggregate numbers for philanthropy in New York City cannot be accurately estimated, but I think it is a safe assertion: New York City's tax base in 1900 could not have funded anything approaching the level of philanthropic activities—cash and services combined—that were provided voluntarily.

Some perspective on this issue is provided by Jacob Riis, whose iconic photographs of the slums of New York documented all that was most terrible about poverty in that era. Today, Riis's work is often used to illustrate the brutality of the Industrial Revolution. Here is the same Jacob Riis, in the same book with those photographs, writing about New York City's response:

> Nowhere is there so eager a readiness to help . . . nowhere are such armies of devoted workers. . . . [New York's] poverty, its slums, and its suffering are the result of unprecedented growth with the consequent disorder and crowding, and the common penalty of metropolitan greatness. . . . [T]he thousand and one charities that in one way or another reach the homes and the lives of the poor with sweetening touch, are proof that if much is yet to be done, if the need only grows with the effort, hearts and hands will be found to do it in ever-increasing measure.[91]

The correct question to ask about dealing with human needs in the twenty-first century is: What if the same proportional level of effort went into civil society's efforts to deal with human needs at today's level of national wealth?

I urge interested readers to pursue the story of the voluntary associations—they represent an extraordinary, largely forgotten accomplishment.[92] Here, I make a limited point. At the time the New Deal began, mutual assistance for insurance did not consist of a few isolated workingmen's groups. Philanthropy to the poor did not consist of a few Lady Bountifuls distributing food baskets. Broad networks, engaging people from the top to bottom of society, spontaneously formed by ordinary citizens, provided sophisticated and effective social insurance and social services of every sort. They did so not just in rural towns or small cities, but in the largest and most impersonal of megalopolises. When I express confidence that under the UBI such networks will regenerate, it is based on historical precedent about how Americans left to themselves tackle social needs, not on wishful thinking.

This leaves open the question of whether it is better to let civil society handle these efforts. It may be argued that it is better to have paid bureaucracies deal with social problems. That way, the burden is not left to people who choose to help, but shared among all the taxpayers. Furthermore, it is more convenient to have bureaucracies do it. Being a part-time social worker appeals to some people, but most of us would rather pay our taxes and be done with it. Perhaps we should concentrate on improving the government bureaucracies that deal with these problems, not dismantling them.

The benefits of returning these functions to civil society are of two kinds: Benefits for the recipients of assistance, and benefits for the rest of us.

The Benefits for Recipients

People trying to help those in need must struggle with a dilemma that the economists call *moral hazard*. People who are in need through no fault of their own can be given generous assistance with no downside risk. But people who are in need at least partly because of their own behavior pose a problem: How to relieve their distress without making it more likely that they will continue to behave in the ways that brought on their difficulties, and without sending the wrong signal to other people who might be tempted.

Bureaucracies have no answer to this dilemma. They cannot distinguish between people who need a pat on the back and those who need a stern warning. They cannot provide help to people who have behaved irresponsibly in a way that does not make it easier for others to behave irresponsibly. Bureaucracies must by their nature be morally indifferent. Indeed, the advocates of the welfare state hold up the moral neutrality of the bureaucracy as one of its advantages because aid is provided without stigma. In contrast, not only are private organizations free to combine moral instruction with the help they give, but such moral instruction is often a primary motivation for the people who are doing the work. Religious belief is sometimes its basis, but the point of view emerges in secular organizations as well. If the recipients of the help are approached as independent moral agents, and if their behavior has contributed to their problems, then the provision of assistance must be linked with attempts to get them to change their ways, subtle or overt.

The result is that private philanthropies tend to provide help in ways that minimize moral hazard. Sometimes moral hazard is reduced because a social penalty accompanies the help. The Florence Crittendon Homes for unwed mothers, for instance, provided help, but moral neutrality about getting pregnant without a husband was not part of the package. Sometimes moral hazard is reduced because the outlook and behavior of the person receiving the assistance are changed for the better. In either case, private charities have the advantage over bureaucracies if the objective is not just to minister to needs, but to discourage the need from arising.

Bureaucracies are also inferior to private philanthropy because a bureaucracy's highest interest cannot help being its own welfare. A new employee may enter a bureaucracy as idealistic as any volunteer, but those who thrive and advance will be those who advance the bureaucracy's interests most effectively. In the business sector, that means growing by gaining new customers and being profitable. For a government bureaucracy, it means growing by increasing its budget and staff.

The institutional interests that drove private philanthropy before the government took a role were the opposite. Charitable organizations had to attract volunteers and donors. The way to attract volunteers was by providing satisfying work for volunteers—which meant the kind of work that the organization was set up to do in the first place, not bureaucratic paper shuffling. The way to attract donors was being able to assure them that their money went to the organization's clients, not to support a large administrative staff. Private charitable organizations had no choice but to keep the effectiveness of their work at the forefront of their attention, else they would go out of business.

It is possible to destroy these advantages of private organizations. The United Way seems designed to make supporting charitable services as much like paying taxes as possible. Go to the Ford Foundation, Red Cross, or other wealthy philanthropies, and you will usually find splendid executive offices, bloated administrative staffs, and layers of paperwork. Go instead to any philanthropy that relies on volunteers and a steady stream of small incoming donations, and you will tend to find lean administrative staffs and a continuing focus on the recipients of the assistance. A story is told about a researcher in the 1980s who was comparing the New York City public school system with New York's Roman Catholic parochial schools, which are parsimoniously funded despite the Catholic Church's global wealth. After he had assembled data on the size of the mammoth administrative staff of the public schools, he phoned the head office of the parochial schools, only to be told by the voice on the other end of the phone that they did not keep information on the number of administrative staff. The researcher persisted. Finally, the voice said, "All right. Wait a minute and I'll count."[93]

The Benefits for the Rest of Us

The second large benefit of taking these functions back into our own hands is that turning them over to a bureaucracy means turning over too much of the stuff of life to them. By *stuff of life* I mean the elemental events of birth, death, growing up, raising children, comforting the bereaved, celebrating success, dealing with adversity, applauding the good, and scorning the bad—coping with life as it exists around us in all its richness. The chief defect of the welfare state from this perspective is not that it is inefficient in dealing with social needs (although it often is), nor that it is ineffectual in dealing with them (although it often is), nor even that it often exacerbates the very problems it is supposed to solve (as it often does). The welfare state drains too much of the life from life.

This argument is not an exhortation for us all to become social workers in our spare time. Give the functions back to the community, and enough people will respond. Free riders can be tolerated. Rather, the existence of vital, extensive networks of voluntary associations engaged in dealing with basic social needs benefits all of us for two other reasons.

The Inculcation of Virtue in the Next Generation. The first reason is that the transmission of virtue to the next generation is the indispensable task of a free society. Networks of voluntary associations are an indispensable way of doing so.

The link between virtue and the success of a free society is not theoretical, but tangible and immediate. A free market cannot work unless the overwhelming majority of the population practices good faith in business transactions. Allowing people to adopt any lifestyle they prefer will not work if a culture does not socialize an overwhelming majority of its children to take responsibility for their actions, to understand long-term consequences, and to exercise self-restraint. Ultimately, a free society does not work unless the population shares a basic sense of right and wrong based on virtue classically understood, propounded in similar terms by thinkers as culturally dissimilar as Aristotle and Confucius. As Edmund Burke put it, "Men are qualified for civil liberty in exact proportion to their disposition to put moral chains upon their own appetites. . . . It is ordained in the eternal constitution of things that men of intemperate minds cannot be free. Their passions forge their fetters."[94]

The question then becomes how virtue is acquired. Aristotle's answer is still the right one: Virtue has the characteristics of a habit and of an acquired skill. It is not enough to tell children that they should be honest, compassionate, and generous. They must practice honesty, compassion, and generosity in the same way that they practice a musical instrument or a sport. Nor does the need for practice stop with childhood. People who behave honestly, compassionately, and generously do not think about each individual choice and decide whether in this particular instance to be honest, compassionate, or generous. They do it as a habit.

If this is an accurate description of how virtue is acquired, then transferring human problems to bureaucracies has an indirect consequence that ultimately degrades the society as a whole: Doing so shrinks an arena in which virtues such as generosity and compassion are practiced. It may not be necessary for everyone to become a volunteer social worker to find satisfaction in life, but it is important that people deal with the human needs of others in a way that is an integral part of everyone's life. In a society where the responsibility for coping with human needs is consigned to bureaucracies, the development of virtue in the next generation is impeded. In a society where that responsibility remains with ordinary citizens, the development of virtue in the next generation is invigorated. The role of voluntary associations in fostering virtue was direct and powerful, as Theda Skocpol has described, even in an age when racial and gender segregation were taken for granted. "[M]embership associations may often have restricted membership," she

writes, "but every category of the population combined into similarly organized cross-class federations expressing much the same Judeo-Christian
and patriotic worldviews. Ironically, this had the effect of pulling American citizens together—teaching them shared values and similar citizenship
practices—even when they did not intend to be united."[95]

The Dynamics of Vital Communities. The other reason that the stuff of life
should not be handed over to bureaucracies involves the dynamics through
which communities remain vital or become moribund. Broken down into
constituent parts, vital communities consist of a multitude of affiliations
among people who are drawn to engage with one another. Some of these
affiliations are as simple as shopping at a local store; some are intended for
nothing more than a good time—the backyard barbecue. Some are organi-
zational—serving as a deacon in one's church. The kinds of affiliations that
draw communities together and give them vitality are tendrils that require
something to attach themselves to, some core of functions around which the
affiliations that constitute a vital community can form and grow. When the
government takes away a core function, it takes away poles for those tendrils.
By hiring professional social workers to care for those most in need, it cuts
off nourishment to secondary and tertiary behaviors that have nothing to do
with social work. According to the logic of the social engineer, there is no
causal connection between such apparently disparate events as the establish-
ment of a welfare bureaucracy and the reduced likelihood (after the passage
of some years) that, when someone dies, a neighbor will prepare a casserole
for the bereaved family's dinner. According to the logic I am using, there is a
causal connection of great importance.

—m—

These are my reasons for thinking that the effects of the UBI on civic culture
are likely to be transforming. The grant will put in each individual's hands
the means to take care of himself under ordinary circumstances. But some
will not take care of themselves. Sometimes the reasons will be beyond their
control. Sometimes people are feckless. Most reasons will be somewhere in
between. The responses to the needs posed by these cases will be as flexible
as their causes. The level of wealth available to address these needs will dwarf

the resources that were available to the fraternal and philanthropic networks of a century ago. Nothing stands in the way of the restoration of networks that are appropriate and generous, and that actually solve problems, except the will to put the responsibility for those problems back in our hands.

12

Conclusion

I began by asking you to ignore that the UBI is politically impossible today. I end it by proposing that something very like the UBI is politically inevitable—not next year, but sometime. Two historical forces lead me to this conclusion.

The first is the secular increase in wealth as the American economy just keeps on growing. The figure below shows the history of American GDP since 1900.

Figure 12-1. Per Capita GDP in 2014 Dollars

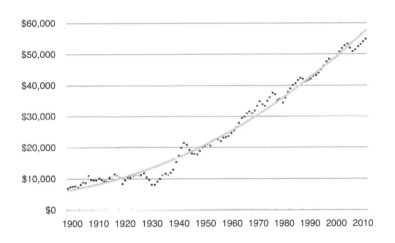

Sources: US Bureau of the Census, 1975, F 1-5; and World Bank.

We may fret about this year's unemployment rate and the effect of a hike in interest rates on economic growth next year, or we may be convinced that the current administration is the worst thing to happen to American economic policy in years, but all of the short-term considerations are swamped by this long-term truth: Real per capita GDP has grown with remarkable consistency for more than a century. It is, of course, possible to elect leaders so incompetent that they will do to the American economy what the Soviet leaders did to theirs, but short of that, we are probably going to watch wealth increase in the decades to come. That curve cannot keep going up for much longer without it becoming obvious to a consensus of the American electorate that lack of money cannot be the reason we have poverty, lack of medical coverage, or an underclass. The problem is that we are spending the money badly.

The second great historical force is the limited competence of government—not our government in particular, or the welfare state in particular, but any government. The limits do not arise because bureaucrats are lazy or the laws improperly written, but from truths about what human beings do when they are not forced to behave in ways that elicit the voluntary cooperation of other people. If constructed with great care, it is possible to have a government that administers a competent military, police, and courts. Even accomplishing this much is demanding. Few countries are fully successful. Every step beyond these simplest, most basic tasks is fraught with increasing difficulty. By the time the government begins trying to administer to complex human needs, it is far out of its depth. Individuals and groups acting privately, with no choice but to behave in ways that elicit voluntary cooperation, do these jobs better. The limited competence of government is inherent. At some point in this century, that too will become a consensus understanding.

Once enough people recognize these realities, the way will be open for reform. What was clear to the founders will once again become clear to a future generation: The greatness of the American project was that it set out to let everyone live life as each person saw fit, as long as each accorded the same freedom to everyone else.

America could not reach that goal as long as the fatal flaw of slavery persisted. When the goal came into sight in the 1960s, we lost our focus and then lost ground. Sometime in the twenty-first century it will become possible to take up the task again, more expansively than the founders could have dreamed but seeking the same end: taking our lives back into our own hands—ours as individuals, ours as families, and ours as communities.

Acknowledgments

In Our Hands is dedicated to Joan Kennedy Taylor, who, in the autumn of 1982, phoned me from out of the blue. She told me she was the director of publications at the Manhattan Institute, and asked whether I was interested in expanding an article I had written for *The Public Interest* into a book. I was, and the book became *Losing Ground.* My gratitude goes as well to William Hammett, the Manhattan Institute's president, who had also read the article and encouraged Joan to get hold of me. His young institute was operating on a shoestring in those days, but Bill found a way to get me a $33,000 advance on royalties and thereby made the project possible.

Twenty-one years later, I got another call from out of the blue, this one from my old friend Irwin Stelzer, who informed me that he knew the title of my next book even though he didn't know what would be in it. I had been writing about social problems for long enough that it was time for me to write my own *What Is To Be Done*, Irwin said, following in Lenin's footsteps.

Irwin had inspired a book idea once before, for *Human Accomplishment*, a book so difficult and exhausting to write that I instinctively recoiled from any new plan he had in mind for me. But as it happened, I did have something I wanted to say about policy solutions. I am a libertarian, but for many years I had thought there ought to be some way to extend a hand across the political divide between libertarians and social democrats, offering a compromise that provided generous assistance for dealing with human needs without entailing the suffocating and soulless welfare state. Milton Friedman's concept of a negative income tax appealed to me as the basis for that compromise. In the late 1980s, I had even written a draft of an article laying out a plan for a revised NIT, but put it away because I could not design it as I wished and still make it affordable. As I reconsidered the issue in 2003, I realized that the intervening years had given the government a lot more money to work with. The technical problems that had vexed me in the late 1980s could be solved.

Thanks go to colleagues at the American Enterprise Institute who read drafts and offered help of many kinds, chief among them Chris DeMuth, Joe Antos, Doug Besharov, Karlyn Bowman, Nick Eberstadt, and Kevin Hassett. Wilson Taylor and Stephen Hyde contributed their specialized expertises to the chapter on health care. Two experts on Social Security, Andrew Biggs and Derrick Max, helped me navigate the rocks and shoals of that daunting system. John Skar contributed his actuarial expertise to an overall review of the numbers. Sam Thernstrom and Lisa Parmelee contributed meticulous editorial assistance and inspired many improvements to the text.

Policy scholars John Cogan, Sheldon Danziger, and Robert Haveman read the penultimate draft and offered critiques from their varying perspectives. Their criticisms prompted dozens of revisions, a few thousand words of new text, and a new appendix—improvements all, although not ones that will reconcile them to an approach that they reject. Sheldon and Bob, who are good social democrats, have my particular thanks for their collegiality in a polarized age. As in all of my endeavors, I must emphasize that just because someone has helped me with my work does not imply endorsement of any part of the result.

Sitting at a desk beside me when I took that call from Joan Taylor in 1982 was my new girlfriend, Catherine Cox. As I write, she is sitting at a desk about 50 feet away from me—now wife, mother of our children, and my most demanding editor. But not even an editor as brilliant as she can give me the words to express the love I feel.

Charles Murray
Burkittsville, Maryland
November 1, 2005

Appendixes

Appendix A
The Programs to Be Eliminated

Data on programs to be eliminated are from three broad categories: Federal transfers to individuals, federal transfers to favored groups, and state and local transfers of both kinds. This appendix details which programs are involved and their cost as of 2014.

Federal Transfers to Individuals

Recent editions of the historical budget tables for the federal budget published annually by the Office of Management and Budget (OMB) have conveniently included a set of tables that are devoted to "outlays for payments to individuals."[96] I exclude certain categories because they involve retirement payments for government employees or benefits for veterans of the armed forces, which I treat as part of the normal personnel costs of a government. The programs with transfers to individuals to be eliminated are listed in the table on the following two pages.

Table A-1. Federal Transfer Payments to Be Eliminated

PROGRAM	OUTLAYS IN 2014 (millions)
Social Security and railroad retirement:	
Old age and survivors insurance	$702,494
Disability insurance	$141,864
Railroad retirement (excluding Social Security)	$8,803
Unemployment assistance	$43,504

(continued on the next page)

Table A-1. Federal Transfer Payments to Be Eliminated (continued)

PROGRAM	OUTLAYS IN 2014 (millions)
Medical care:	
Medicare: hospital insurance	$262,569
Medicare: supplementary medical insurance	$322,430
Children's health insurance	$9,317
Medicaid	$301,472
Indian health	$4,510
Health resources and services	$7,604
Substance abuse and mental health services	$3,193
Center for Medicare and Medicaid Innovation	$997
Refundable Premium Tax Credit and Cost Sharing Reductions	$13,068
Pre-Existing Condition Insurance Plan Program	$535
Early Retiree Reinsurance	$13
Other health care	$12,286
Assistance to students	$56,337
Housing assistance	$46,600
Food and nutrition assistance:	
SNAP (formerly food stamps) (including Puerto Rico)	$76,237
Child nutrition and special milk programs	$19,490
Supplemental feeding programs (WIC and CSFP)	$6,266
Commodity donations and other	$823
Public assistance and related programs:	
Supplemental Security Income program	$51,499
Family support payments to states and TANF	$20,378
Low-income home energy assistance	$3,537
Earned income tax credit	$60,087
Payments to states for day care assistance	$5,064
Payments to states—foster care/adoption assistance	$6,868
Payment where child credit exceeds tax liability	$21,490
Refundable AMT credit	$67
Other public assistance	$1,004
All other payments for individuals:	
Coal miners and black lung benefits	$426
Aging services programs	$1,462
Energy employees compensation fund	$1,052
September 11th victim compensation	$49
Refugee assistance and other	$4,403
TOTAL	**$2,213,395**

Source: OMB-HB, Table 11.3.

The bulk of the money to finance a UBI would come from just three programs of transfers to individuals: Social Security (which includes disability payments as well as pensions), Medicare, and Medicaid. All are unambiguously transfers, and they are huge.[97] In 2014, outlays to pay for them amounted to 72 percent of federal transfers to individuals.

Federal Transfers to Favored Groups

The next set of programs consist of government spending that benefits a specific industry, corporation, nonprofit organization, or an identifiable group of people. Sometimes the group shares an occupation (e.g., farmers), sometimes ethnicity (e.g., American Indians), and sometimes the same geographical setting (e.g., people living in communities selected for block grants). Sometimes the transfer is direct, in the form of grants, loans, or subsidies. In many cases the transfer is implicit, with the government funding a service or applied research for an industry that the industry should be doing for itself if the service or research is worth the cost.

Many of these transfers are embedded deep in the budgets of agencies, and I have not tried to ferret out all of them. For example, the subsidy for Amtrak, found far down the hierarchy in the Department of Transportation's budget, benefits a small proportion of the population, disproportionately those who live along the Northeast corridor from Washington to Boston, but its budget amounts to a few hundred million dollars—chicken feed relative to the more than $2.5 trillion in total transfers. In 2015, the Bureau of Indian Affairs got $2.5 billion tucked in the budget for the Department of the Interior—a lot of money, most of us would think, but less than 0.1 percent of all federal transfers.

Instead of combing through the budgets of every cabinet department and independent agency, I selected the line items from Table 3.2 of OMB's Historical Tables, "Outlays by Function and Subfunction: 1962–2020," that consist primarily of transfers to favored groups. They are listed in the table below.

I use the total of $69.4 billion from these programs as a proxy for a more precise enumeration of transfers to favored groups. Thus I do not include the cost of Amtrak whereas I include all of "area and regional development" even though some expenditures of that program might escape a strict definition of "transfer." Education expenditures are an especially problematic category.

Table A-2 .Federal Transfer Payments to Favored Groups

PROGRAM	OUTLAYS IN 2014 (millions)
Farm income stabilization	$20,012
Agricultural research and services	$4,374
Community development	$7,896
Area and regional development	$3,027
Disaster relief and insurance	$9,747
Training and employment	$7,013
Social services	$17,299
TOTAL	**$54,083**

Source: OMB-HB, Table 3.2.

I accept that education is a classic public good and therefore government expenditures on education need not be seen as transfers. But most federal expenditures on education are selectively targeted to favored groups, whether low-income communities or currently fashionable causes, not to the general funding of education. To simplify defense of my totals, I omitted all expenditures on education except for direct transfers to individual students, and I recommend you take the same approach to your review of the line items in both tables. It's not necessary to spend much time deciding whether you agree that all of them are transfers, nor should you worry much about programs (especially corporate welfare) that might have escaped my notice. Tweaking the set of programs other than the Big Three, adding a few and subtracting a few, would have negligible effect on the total.

State and Local Transfers to Individuals and Favored Groups

The principle behind the UBI is that *all* transfers that take money from the nation's taxpayers and give it to individuals and groups should be consolidated into a single transfer, the UBI. That principle applies to transfers at the state and local level as well.

Data on these expenditures come from the "census of governments" that the Census Bureau conducts every five years (for years ending in two and seven).[98] The most recent was conducted in 2012 and included budget data for fiscal year 2013, when states and localities spent approximately $461 billion of their own money (over and above federal revenues shared with states and localities) for the categories labeled public welfare, health, hospitals, and housing and community development—the categories for which virtually all expenditures consist of cash or in-kind transfers to individuals or favored groups.

The figure of $461 billion is approximate because the published figures from the Census Bureau for the 2012 survey do not include the federal revenues that went specifically to these four categories, instead reporting a total for all federal revenues that went to all categories of state and local spending, plus total spending (combining the federal, state, and local contributions) on the four categories. Given the pattern of the data for earlier years, however, there is reason to think that the figure of $461 billion is quite close to the unknown real one. From 2000 through 2008, when the Census Bureau published the federal contributions to the four categories, those totals constituted a remarkably consistent proportion of all federal contributions—never lower than 61.6 percent and never higher than 63.2 percent, with an average of 62.8 percent. The $461 billion estimate is produced by multiplying the total federal contribution to state and local spending in 2013 by 0.628. Confidence in this estimate is bolstered by a graph of the known state and local contributions from 2000 to 2008 and the estimated figure for 2013, shown in Figure A-1.

The linear trend line in the graph was calculated using fiscal years 2000–2008 when the actual state and local contributions to the four categories were known. The estimate for fiscal year 2013 falls almost precisely on that trend line. I used a linear extrapolation to reach an estimate of $477 billion for 2014, the year I am using for the federal expenditures.

Total Cost of the Current System in 2014

To summarize, here is where the money to fund the UBI would come from:

- Federal transfers to individuals ($2.22 trillion),

Figure A-1. State and Local Transfer Payments, 2000–2013

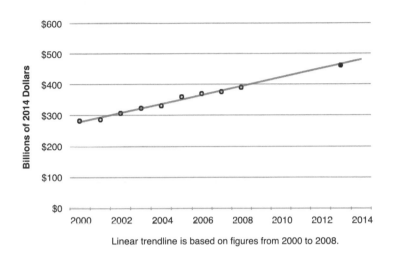

Linear trendline is based on figures from 2000 to 2008.

Sources: For 2000–2008: US Census Bureau, 2013, Table 435, and comparable tables in earlier years. For 2013: US Census Bureau, "State and Local Government Finances by Level of Government and by State: 2012–2013," www.census.gov.

- Federal transfers to favored groups ($69 billion), and

- State and local transfers of all kinds ($477 billion).

Total cost of the programs to be eliminated, using unrounded figures ($2.77 trillion).

Appendix B
The UBI's Cost Compared with
the Cost of the Current System

This appendix lays out the assumptions and choices that underpin the discussion of the UBI's affordability in Chapter 2. The first half of this appendix discusses the costs of the current system from 2000 to 2020; the second half turns to the computation of the costs of the UBI. All figures are stated in constant 2014 dollars.

Past and Projected Costs of the Current System

Figure B-1 below shows the total federal expenditures on transfers under four headings: Federal transfers to the elderly, other federal transfers to individuals (primarily low-income persons, the disabled, and the unemployed), federal transfers to groups, and all state and local transfers to individuals and favored groups.

The money spent on the elderly dominates the calculation of transfer payments and, ominously, is also the category that is projected to show the steepest rise in the future.

Estimating the Cost of the UBI

The UBI grant described in Chapter 2 is set at $13,000 per year, with a progressive surtax that begins at 10 percent for those making $30,000–$34,999 per year and increases by 4-percentage-point increments until it reaches a maximum of 30 percent for those making $55,000–$59,999 per year. Those making $60,000 or more receive half of the grant, $6,500.

Figure B-1. State and Local Transfer Payments, 2000–2013

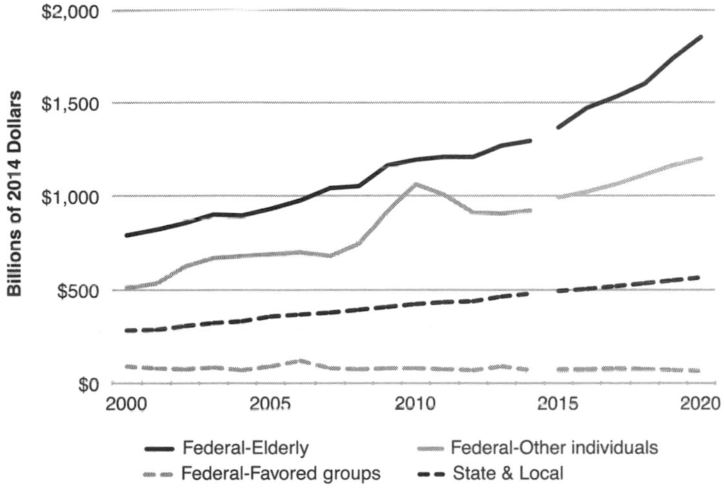

Sources: OMB-HB Tables 3.2 and 11.3; and Census Bureau's Census of Governments, 2007 and 2012.

The annual cost of the UBI depends on the average net amount received by eligible citizens, which in turn depends on income distribution, which in turn is affected by the age distribution. To estimate the costs of the UBI across the years, the following procedure was followed:

1. The Census Bureau's detailed age projections for 2014 to 2060 were used to determine the size of cohorts by age and sex for 2014 to 2020.[99] The age groupings were 21–24, 25–34, 35–44, 45–54, 55–64, 65–74, and 75 and older.

2. The 2015 Current Population Survey was used to determine the income distribution for each age/sex cell in calendar 2014.[100] Those data were used to estimate the average net grant for persons falling within each cell.

3. Those averages were then applied to the comparable population groupings for 2014–2020.

The projected costs of the UBI thus take into account changes in both the sex and age composition of the population, using the assumptions that neither income distribution nor labor force participation change. The result of this procedure is an estimated cost of the UBI in 2014 of $2.58 trillion, which is projected to rise to $2.75 trillion by 2020 and $2.88 trillion by 2025. Chapter 2 discusses the surprisingly small effects that violations of these assumptions have on the total cost of the UBI.

Appendix C
Preliminary Thoughts About Political
Feasibility and Transition Issues

This appendix addresses the question of political feasibility of the UBI, with particular reference to the people in midlife who would have to accept the transition from the current system to the UBI. By *political feasibility* I do not mean whether Congress can be persuaded to pass the UBI. Rather, imagine that somehow the UBI were put to a referendum in which individual Americans were asked to vote it up or down. Does replacing the current system with the UBI ask a significant proportion of the electorate to vote against its own best interests?

For the half of adults who are below the nation's median income, the answer is almost always "no." The UBI offers a much better deal than the current system with the exception of some single mothers over 21 who do not work at all (see Chapters 3 and 5).

The issue of political feasibility centers on two groups: those who are in the upper half of the income distribution, and those who have been contributing to the current system for many years and would get caught in the transition from the current system to the UBI.

The Forgone Benefits from the Current System for Those
in the Top Half of the Income Distribution

In this section, I am comparing people who would be on the current system throughout their adult lives with people who would be on the UBI throughout their adult lives.

The obvious reason that people in the top half of the income distribution might rationally prefer the current system is that they put more money into the Social Security and Medicare programs than they would get back from the grant. As of 2016, an employee and employer are each taxed an amount equal to 6.2 percent of the employee's salary for FICA and another 1.45 percent each for Medicare. The income cap for FICA for 2016 is $118,500. Medicare has no income cap. For a person making exactly $118,500, the direct annual cost is thus $9,065. Since the employer's contribution to Social Security and Medicare is coming out of the pool of money available to pay wages, the real contributions are twice those amounts, but even without adding in the employer's contribution, all people making more than $84,967 are putting more into the current system than the $6,500 they will take out of the UBI.

Furthermore, the UBI does not offer them the carrot of being freed from FICA and Medicare taxes because the financial feasibility of the UBI is based on the assumption that total government revenues will be the same as they would be under the current system. There is no way to reconfigure the tax system so that middle-income and affluent citizens do not end up paying just about as much tax as they do now. The first question thus becomes what benefits they are giving up under the current system, and the second question is how much they would get back under the UBI.

The Dollar Value of the Benefits of the Current System for the Middle Class on Up. Comparatively few people in the top half of the income distribution get much from welfare programs, unemployment insurance, or the many other transfers focused on low-income individuals. Few of them get much from corporate welfare (see the line for federal transfers to favored groups in Figure B-1 in Appendix B). When people with incomes above the national median ask themselves how they should vote in the referendum on the UBI, they're thinking primarily about what it means to give up their prospective Social Security and Medicare benefits.

In 2015, people retiring at the full retirement age of 66 who paid maximum FICA taxes for at least 35 years got $2,263 per month, or almost $32,000 per year. The dollar value of the Medicare benefit depends on personal utility functions that will vary from person to person. As a benchmark, I use Medicare benefit payments per enrollee per year. In the most recent available data, for 2013, that figure was about $11,200.[101]

Adding Social Security and Medicare, retired Americans who contributed the maximum payroll taxes throughout their working lives thus got about $43,200 in benefits from the current system in 2015. Those in the top half of the income distribution who paid less than the maximum for a significant portion of their working lives got somewhat less, and those who deferred taking Social Security until they were older than 66 got somewhat more, but I will use the $43,200 as the point of reference. The comparative advantage of the UBI that I am about to demonstrate is even greater for those who got less than $43,200.

The Dollar Value of the UBI for the Middle Class on Up. As noted, all adults who make more than $84,967 would be paying more payroll taxes or their equivalent than the $6,500 net they would get from the UBI. Why should they support the UBI?

The answer exposes how inefficient the current system is: Even while paying in more than the $6,500 the government gives back during their working years, they can expect to be much better off under the UBI when the time comes to retire. To illustrate, take someone who graduates from college at 21 and immediately gets a job paying more than $60,000 a year, and therefore never gets more than the $6,500 minimum. He spends the $3,000 on the catastrophic health care policy, leaving just $3,500 from the grant, which he invests annually in a retirement account that returns the standard 4 percent I assumed in Chapter 4. When he retires at age 66, he will have about $440,000, a sum that will purchase an annuity of about $30,200. If he were to have no other retirement income whatsoever, his net retirement package would be $40,180 ($30,200 from the annuity plus $9,980 cash[102] from the UBI), $8,180 more than the $32,000 he can expect from Social Security under the current system, plus his catastrophic health care package. Even if he spent all of the $8,180 extra on supplemental health insurance care to match Medicare benefits, he would be getting as much from the UBI as he gets from the current system

But that's not the end of a sensible young person's calculations. Four percent is a minimal return. Hardly any of these same young people who expect to be making more than $60,000 would think it realistic to assume that they will get so little from their stock portfolio over the long term. And they're right. As discussed in Chapter 3, if you invest your money in a fund indexed to the stock market for 45 years and get only a 4 percent return, you will have gotten less than you would have gotten from any 45-year period in the history of the United States.

Suppose that our young man gets the average for the most recent 45-year period, a 6.1 percent annual real return over that 45 years. In that case, his accumulation will be about $829,000, purchasing an annuity worth about $57,000 per year. Add in the continuing grant of $6,500, and he is getting $63,500 in retirement income compared with the $32,000 he can expect from Social Security. He can buy a lot of supplemental health insurance with the extra money to close the difference between his catastrophic health insurance and Medicare. So, as our 21-year-old looks to the future, the UBI promises benefits marginally better than the current system even if he is extremely unlucky, and a big bonus if he lives in a merely average economic era.

So far, I am assuming that our young man will remain single all his life. If instead he marries, the prospective benefits of the UBI for him and his wife double if she works full time at a similarly remunerative job. They are also far greater even if she is a full-time homemaker because she generates a substantial retirement income of her own that would not have existed at all under the current system. More generally, if we are talking about a 21-year-old choosing between the current system or the UBI, even those who expect to be above the national median income get a better deal under the UBI.

Let me take this to an extreme. Suppose we have a 21-year-old who says to himself, "I'm really stupid with money. I won't save any. I'll make bad investments. I will reach retirement with nothing but my $10,000 a year. Therefore I prefer to stick with the current system." He is not being rational. If he is able to think that about himself in that way at age 21, the rational next step is to say, "Therefore I will sign an irrevocable contract that commits $3,500 from my annual grant, divided among several conservative investment firms, for investment in index-based portfolios." The only way that the current system could be rationally preferred by an affluent 21-year-old is if he could expect the next 45 years to be economically the worst in American history and that, in spite of this, the current system could continue to make good on its obligations—an impossible combination. I have said it before in this book, but it bears repeating and italicizing: *The current system cannot meet its obligations if the American economy does not continue to grow at a rate that would produce the minimal private returns assumed by the UBI.*

Transition Issues

If the UBI were actually to be implemented, policymakers would have to fig-ure out how to deal with those who have been playing by the current system's rules with expectations about the current system's payoffs. The simplest solu-tion would be to offer everyone who is in mid-career or older a free choice to stay with the current system or switch to the UBI. As throughout the book, I assume no tax effects: aside from the surtax on the UBI itself, the federal tax burden currently made up of payroll taxes and the income tax does not change.

What transition costs would this entail? To calculate a technically sound estimate would probably take a team of economists months of work. It involves complex modeling and the acquisition of detailed economic and demographic data on a wide variety of issues. Here, I have a more mod-est purpose: to demonstrate that extremely large numbers of Americans in mid-career or older would choose the UBI even though they have been pay-ing into Social Security and Medicare for many years. Here are few specific examples in support of that proposition:

Middle-Aged Upper-Middle-Class Households with Two Incomes Pay-ing the Maximum Surtax. Let's start with people who are starting to think about retirement and have spent their adult lives contributing to the current system. Specifically, consider the situation of an upper-middle-class couple who are both age 50 when the switch to the UBI arrives. They both work, and have been earning the maximum Social Security wage base all of their working lives. If they continue doing so until they retire at 66, they will each get the maximum Social Security benefit as of 2015, totaling about $64,000 as a couple. If their health is average, they will each take out about $11,200 per year in Medicare benefits starting at age 65.

At age 50, the average person can expect to live for another 31.5 years (more if a woman, less if a man; I'll simplify and use the average).[103] If they both die on schedule at 81.5, they will have received 16.5 years of Social Security benefits, totaling $1,056,000 in cash, plus medical benefits that have an expected value of $369,600. Why on earth should they consider giving that up to participate in the UBI?

The surprising answer is that they could easily prefer to give up both Social Security and Medicare and switch to the UBI even at that late date.

The explanation is that the priorities of a middle-aged upper-middle class couple are likely to be far different from the priorities of people who depend on Social Security for their retirement.

A couple in which both members are paying the maximum payroll tax for Social Security is making at least two times $118,500, or $237,000. If they have been making the maximum contribution throughout their careers, they are unlikely to be paying attention to the prospective size of their Social Security income after they retire, because it is minor compared with the value of the assets they will have accumulated and is unlikely to make a difference in their lifestyle. Similarly, they could afford their own health insurance if Medicare disappeared under any circumstances, but with no trouble at all if the costs of individual health care and group health care have been equalized through the single-pool rule.

The first question in their minds is what the combined $13,000 per year in cash ($6,500 each) that the UBI would bring them can do for their net worth. They are already carrying medical insurance that more than meets the requirements for catastrophic health coverage. So in effect the UBI will annually give them $13,000 in extra cash that they can put into their investment portfolio.

If they expect a normal return—I'll stay with the 6.1 percent return for 1970–2014—instead of the worst case from the stock market, they will expect to have accumulated more than $1.2 million through the UBI when they both drop dead 31.5 years later. Which is preferable? $1.2 million added to their estate or the $1.1 million in Social Security payments plus Medicare benefits? Different couples will make different choices. But it's a close call even though they are entering the UBI and foregoing Social Security and Medicare at age 50.

Obviously, all of the parameters in this exercise are subject to alteration. The expected return could be changed from 6.1 percent, Medicare could be valued differently, or the prospective use of Social Security payments under the current system could include an investment component. The point of the example is not proof, but illustration. Even just 16 years away from retirement, after having paid the maximum into Social Security and Medicare since their first job, the choice between moving to the UBI or staying in the current system is likely to be close even if the government offers no compensation at all for giving up their right to Social Security and Medicare benefits. Now think how much more attractive the UBI comes for two-income affluent couples even a few years younger than 50.

Middle-Aged Upper-Middle-Class Households with One Income Paying the Maximum Surtax. Now reconsider that same couple at age 50—same total household income, same household private retirement income—with just one difference: This has always been a one-income household; the wife has never worked outside the home, and she will therefore get no Social Security, knocking $32,000 off the couple's retirement income under the current system. The UBI specifies that someone without income gets the full grant, no matter what the spouse makes. Thus, instead of getting a combined UBI of $13,000 a year to invest, the affluent one-income family gets $19,500 ($13,000 + $6,500, on the assumption that an affluent couple already has health insurance meeting the catastrophic health insurance requirement). For this couple, the expected accumulation by the time they die is about $1.9 million, compared with the couple's expected benefits from Social Security of $528,000 plus Medicare.

Middle-Aged Working-Class Households with $60,000 from Two Incomes. What about transition costs for people further down the income ladder? In this example, both members of the couple are again 50, planning to retire at 66, but are each making exactly $30,000 when they are asked if they want to switch to the UBI. Their expected Social Security income when they retire will be $14,000 each, or $28,000 total.[104]

Unlike the affluent couple, this working-class couple depends on Social Security as the major source of their retirement income. After buying their required catastrophic health insurance, the UBI will give them $20,000 per year in additional cash, but they have too many demands on living expenses to use all of it to put into a retirement fund. Instead, the two of them combined use half of it, $10,000 per year, for their retirement fund.

By the time they retire at 66, they expect to have accumulated about $270,00, which will get them an annuity paying $18,528 per year. Adding in their $20,000 cash from the continuing UBI, they thus have a total retirement income of $38,528 per year, compared with the $28,000 they would have gotten from Social Security. After using some of the surplus to augment their health insurance, transferring to the UBI at age 50 is roughly equal to the advantages of sticking with the existing combination of Social Security and Medicare.

Middle-Aged Low-Income Households with $30,000 from One Income.
Moving to people who are near the poverty line, consider a couple who are both again 50, planning to retire at 66, but only one is working, making exactly $30,000 when they are asked if they want to switch to the UBI. Their expected Social Security income when they retire will be just $14,000. After buying their required catastrophic health insurance, the UBI will give them $20,000 per year in additional cash, but they, like the working-class family, have too many demands on living expenses to use all of it to replace the value of their lost Social Security and Medicare. The two of them together manage to contribute only $5,000 per year into their retirement fund.

By the time the wage-earner retires, they expect to have accumulated about $135,000, which buys an annuity worth $9,264 per year. Their total retirement income under the UBI is thus $29,264, compared with $14,000 under the current system. Once again, transferring to the UBI makes sense.

The Bottom Line

The permutations are numerous: spouses who once worked and have now stopped working, one spouse with a large salary and another with a small one—all of which produce different results. The common theme is that the UBI is so superior to the current system under such a broad range of assumptions about future economic growth that large proportions of people even in their 50s, let alone younger, will rationally choose the UBI despite the investment they have already made into Social Security and Medicare until then. Nothing in this analysis denies that the transition from the current system to the UBI would pose many practical problems. But neither should we refuse to consider the UBI because the transition would be unmanageably difficult.

Bibliography

Anderson, E. 1993. "Sex Codes and Family Life Among Poor Inner-City Youths." In *Young Unwed Fathers: Changing Roles and Emerging Policies*, ed. R. I. Lerman and T. J. Ooms. Philadelphia: Temple University Press, 74–98.

Bartholet, E. 1999. *Nobody's Children: Abuse and Neglect, Foster Drift, and the Adoption Alternative*. Boston: Beacon Press.

Beito, D. T. 2000. *From Mutual Aid to the Welfare State: Fraternal Societies and Social Services, 1890–1967*. Chapel Hill, NC: University of North Carolina Press.

———. 2002. This Enormous Army. *In the Voluntary City: Choice, Community, and Civil Society*, ed. D. T. Beito, P. Gordon, and A. Tabarrok. Ann Arbor, MI: University of Michigan Press.

Brooks, A. C. 2015. *The Conservative Heart: How to Build a Fairer, Happier, and More Prosperous America*. New York: Broadside Books.

Brooks, R. G., N. Menachemi, C. Hughes, and A. Clawson. 2004. "Impact of the Medical Professional Liability Insurance Crisis on Access to Care in Florida." *Archives of Internal Medicine* 164: 2217–22.

Burke, E. 1791. Letter to a Member of the National Assembly. In *The Maxims and Reflections of Burke*, ed. F. W. Rafferty, www.ourcivilisation.com.

Burkhauser, R. V., and T. A. Finegan. 1993. "The Economics of Minimum Wage Legislation Revisited." *Cato Journal* 13 (1): 123–29.

Butrica, B. A., K. E. Smith, and H. M. Iams. 2012. "This Is Not Your Parents' Retirement: Comparing Retirement Income Across Generations." *Social Security Bulletin* 72 (1): 37–58.

Cain, G. G., and D. A. Wissoker. 1990. "A Reanalysis of Marital Stability in the Seattle-Denver Income-Maintenance Experiment." *American Journal of Sociology* 95: 1235–69.

Cowan, T. 2013. *Average Is Over: Powering America Beyond the Age of the Great Stagnation*. New York: Dutton.

DuBois, W. E. B. [1899] 1967. *The Philadelphia Negro: A Social Study*. New York: Benjamin Blom.

Eberstadt, N. 2008. *The Poverty of the Poverty Rate: Measure and Mismeasure of Material Deprivation in Modern America*. Washington, DC: AEI Press.

Freeman, R. B. 1999. "The Economics of Crime." In *Handbook of Labor Economics*, ed. O. Ashenfelter and D. Card, vol. 3. New York: Elsevier Science, 3529–71.

Friedman, M. 1962. *Capitalism and Freedom*. Chicago: University of Chicago Press.

Frejka, T., and Sobotka, T. 2008. "Fertility in Europe: Diverse, Delayed and Below Replacement." *Demographic Research*, 19 (3), 15–45.

Gutman, H. G. 1976. *The Black Family in Slavery and Freedom 1750–1925*. New York: Vintage Books.

Hannan, M. T., and N. B. Tuma. 1990. "A Reassessment of the Effect of Income Maintenance on Marital Dissolution in the Seattle-Denver Experiment." *American Journal of Sociology* 95: 1270–98.

Herrnstein, R. J. 1997. *The Matching Law: Papers in Psychology and Economics.* Cambridge, MA: Harvard University Press.

Herrnstein, R. J., and C. Murray. 1994. *The Bell Curve: Intelligence and Class Structure in American Life.* New York: Free Press.

Kessler, D., and M. McClellan. 1996. "Do Doctors Practice Defensive Medicine?" *Quarterly Journal of Economics* 111 (2): 353–90.

Lampman, R. 1965. "Approaches to the Reduction of Poverty." *American Economic Review* 55: 521–29.

Levitt, S. D. 2004. "Understanding Why Crime Fell in the 1990s: Four Factors That Explain the Decline and Six That Do Not." *Journal of Economic Perspectives* 18 (1): 163–90.

Lovejoy, A. O. 1961. *Reflections on Human Nature.* Baltimore, MD: Johns Hopkins University Press.

McLanahan, S. 1999. "Father Absence and the Welfare of Children." In *Coping with Divorce, Single Parenting, and Remarriage: A Risk and Resiliency Perspective,* ed. M. Hetherington. Mahwah, NJ: Lawrence Erlbaum Associates.

McLanahan, S., and G. Sandefur. 1994. *Growing Up with a Single Parent.* Cambridge, MA: Harvard University Press.

McLanahan, S., E. Donahue, and R. Haskins, eds. 2005. *Marriage and Child Wellbeing,* vol. 2 Washington, DC: Brookings Institution.

Miettinen, A., A. Rotkirch, I. Szalma, A. Donno, and M.-L. Tanturri. 2015. *Increasing Childlessness in Europe: Time Trends and Country Differences.* www.familiesandsocieties.eu

Murray, C. 1984. Losing Ground: *American Social Policy, 1950–1980.* New York: Basic Books.

———. 1988. *In Pursuit: Of Happiness and Good Government.* New York: Simon and Schuster.

———. 1994. What to Do About Welfare. *Commentary.* December.

———. 1997. *What It Means to Be a Libertarian: A Personal Interpretation.* New York: Broadway Books.

———. 1999. *The Underclass Revisited.* Washington, DC: AEI Press.

———. 2012. *Coming Apart: The State of White America, 1960–2010.* New York: Crown Forum.

Olasky, M. 1992. *The Tragedy of American Compassion.* Washington, DC: Regnery Gateway.

Perelli-Harris, B., W. Sigle-Rushton, M. Kreyenfeld, T. Lappegard, C. Berghammer, and R. Keizer. 2010. *The Educational Gradient of Nonmarital Childbearing in Europe: Emergence of a Pattern of Disadvantage?* www.rug.nl/research.

Piehl, A. M. 1998. "Economic Conditions, Work, and Crime." In *The Handbook of Crime and Punishment,* ed. M. Tonry, 302–19. New York: Oxford University Press.

Pollock, I. L. 1923. *The Food Administration in Iowa,* vol. 1. Iowa City: State Historical Society of Iowa.

Rhee, S. H., and I. D. Waldman. 2002. Genetic and Environmental Influences on Antisocial Behavior: A Meta-Analysis of Twin and Adoption Studies. *Psychological Bulletin* 128 (3): 490–529.

Rifkin, J. 2004. *The European Dream: How Europe's Vision of the Future Is Quietly Eclipsing the American Dream.* New York: Penguin.

Riis, J. 1890. *How the Other Half Lives: Studies Among the Tenements of New York.* New York: Charles Scribner's Sons. www.yale.edu/amstud/inforev/riis/title.html (accessed October 4, 2005).

Shaw, G. B. 1916. *Pygmalion.* drama.eserver.org.

Siegel, J. 1998. *Stocks for the Long Run: The Definitive Guide to Financial Market Returns and Long-Term Investment Strategies,* 2nd ed. New York: McGraw-Hill.

Simon, H. A. 1956. Rational Choice and the Structure of the Environment. *Psychological Review,* 63 (2), 128–138.

Skocpol, T. 2003. *Diminished Democracy: From Membership to Management in American Life.* Norman, Okla.: University of Oklahoma Press.

Smith, A. [1759] 1979. *The Theory of Moral Sentiments.* http://oll.libertyfund.org.

Stigler, G. 1946. The Economics of Minimum Wage Legislation. *American Economic Review* 36 (June): 358–65.

Studdert, D. M., M. M. Mello, and T. A. Brennan. 2004. Medical Malpractice. *New England Journal of Medicine* 350: 283–92.

Sullivan, M. L. 1993. Young Fathers and Parenting in Two Inner-City Neighborhoods. In *Young Unwed Fathers: Changing Roles and Emerging Policies,* ed. R. I. Lerman and T. J. Ooms. Philadelphia: Temple University Press, 52–73.

Tocqueville, A. de. [1835] 1969. *Democracy in America.* http://oll.libertyfund.org.

Van IJzendoorn, M., F. Juffer, and C. Poelhuis. 2005. Adoption and Cognitive Development: A Meta-Analytic Comparison of Adopted and Nonadopted Children's IQ and School Performance. *Psychological Bulletin* 131 (2): 301–16.

Walzer, M. 1983. *Spheres of Justice: A Defense of Pluralism and Equality.* New York: Basic Books.

Westoff, C. F., and Frejka, T. (2007). Religiousness and Fertility Among European Muslims. *Population and Development Review,* 33 (4), 785–809.

Wilcox, W. B., ed. 2011. *Why Marriage Matters, Third Edition: Thirty Conclusions from the Social Sciences.* New York: Broadway Publications.

Wilson, J. Q. 1993. *The Moral Sense.* New York: The Free Press.

Zong, J., and Batalova, J. 2015. Frequently Requested Statistics on Immigrants and Immigration in the United States. Migration Policy Institute. www.migrationpolicy.org.

Notes

I did not try to update all the sources in the endnotes for the 2016 edition. Recent work as been done on all of these topics, and in a few cases I cite new titles, but the state of knowledge has seldom changed dramatically since 2006. Almost all of the sources in the original version are as pertinent now as they were a decade ago.

For sources taken from the Internet, I give the website's name and the URL for the home page. I do not give the specific Web page because websites change their indexes frequently. Nor do I include the date when I accessed the website; if the page no longer exists when you read the book, knowing that it did at some particular date in the past does not seem helpful. The full citations of government documents are given in the notes. The bibliography is reserved for books, journal articles, and other scholarly works.

The following abbreviations are used for data sources that are referenced frequently in the text:

CPS. The Current Population Survey, sponsored jointly by the Census Bureau and the Bureau of Labor Statistics, is the federal government's primary survey for tracking income and labor force statistics and is also used a wide variety of demographic analysis. The CPS surveys going back to 1962 are downloadable from the Minnesota Population Center's website, cps.ipums.org. Citations in the text are "CPS" followed by the year. The most frequently cited version is CPS-2015.

OMB-HB. Office of Management and Budget historical budgets. This website, www.whitehouse.gov/omb/budget/historicals, has budget data going all the way back to 1789, with the most complete data series beginning in 1940. The tables used for the 2016 edition of *In Our Hands* have actual budget figures through 2014 and projected budget figures for 2015 to 2020.

Preface

1. Cowan (2013). See also Scott Santens, "Deep Learning Is Going to Teach Us All the Lesson of Our Lives: Jobs Are for Machines," Medium, March 16, 2016, medium.com/basic-income.

Introduction

2. The long version is Murray (1988). The short version is Murray (1997).

Chapter 1: The Plan

3. The article was Stigler (1946). Stigler revealed that the idea came from Friedman in later correspondence. Burkhauser and Finegan (1993), 128.

4. Friedman (1962), 191–94.

5. Lampman (1965).

6. For a summary of the results of the NIT experiment, see Murray (1984), chap. 11.

7. The statement in the text is true for the official poverty rate. The official measure is a bad one. It has failed to capture many aspects of material poverty that actually have declined and, equally, masks indicators that the proportion of Americans who would be poor without government support has increased. See Eberstadt (2008) for the former argument and Murray (1999) for the latter.

8. Many advocates for a guaranteed income on the left call their plans BIG, for Basic Income Guarantee. I have a substantive reason for labeling my plan UBI instead. Plans from the left always treat the guaranteed income as an add-on to the existing array of social services and income supplements provided by the state. I think such plans would be worse than the status quo. Achieving my main goals for a guaranteed income absolutely require that it *replace* those social services and income supplements, for reasons that are explained throughout the book. I use the label UBI instead of BIG to emphasize this distinction between my plan and those from the left. And because I think BIG is too cute.

9. Would it be necessary to revoke automatic citizenship for babies born in the United States? Not really. The parents of the baby have to wait 21 years before either they or their child get the UBI. In the meantime, they have to get along in a United States in which the entire welfare state has been dismantled.

10. If so desired, the amount of the grant could be adjusted monthly, based on income-to-date in that calendar year, with a year-end adjustment to correct for over or underpayments because of unusual fluctuations in income.

11. If this option were used, the definition of median earned income would have to be based on the median for the entire population age 21 and over, not the median for people with income, so that changes in labor force participation would be reflected in lowered median income.

Chapter 2: Basic Finances

12. In 2013, about 13 percent of the population were immigrants, legal and illegal, of whom about 53 percent were not citizens. Of those, approximately 80 percent were over 21, representing about 18 million people. Zong and Batalova (2015). In the same year, 2.2 million adults were incarcerated in federal prisons, state prisons, and county jails, about 2 million of whom were 21 or older. See E. A. Carson, "Prisoners in 2013," NCJ 247282, US Department of Justice, Office of Justice Programs, Bureau of Justice Statistics, September 16, 2014, www.bjs.gov/index.cfm?ty=pbdetail&iid=5109.

13. Theoretically, Medicaid costs could be significantly changed if there were a major reduction or increase in poverty, but even the level of poverty has moved within a narrow range since the early 1970s. In practice, Medicaid costs are also on a persistent trend line.

14. Historical data on employment and labor force participation are available at the Bureau of Labor Statistics website, www.bls.gov, in Table 1 of its annual Employment & Earnings Online publication. Median personal income is based on the author's analysis of the CPS-2015.

15. Formally, this represents the cost if a grant equivalent to $13,000 in 2014 dollars had been used for the plan presented in the 2006 edition, based on the income distribution of 2002 and the population of 2014.

Chapter 3: Health Care

16. Author's analysis, American Community Survey 2008–2012 five-year sample, https://usa.ipums.org/usa/.

17. When I wrote the original version of In Our Hands, a few pioneering versions of these clinics had just gotten started. Since then, services of the kind I have in mind have become more widespread. For example, most drug store chains offer flu shots and other vaccinations. Regulations still prevent them from taking on more than a fraction of the medical services that they should be able to offer. But even if they were freed of stifling regulations, their popularity would be limited as long as the actual out-of-pocket cost of a visit to a MinuteClinic and to one's personal physician remained the same, as it often does with employer-provided insurance, Medicare, or Medicaid.

18. The source for the original data was the Center to Advance Palliative Care, www. capcmssm.org, which remains a good source. For some specific current numbers, see Helen Adamopoulos, "The Cost and Quality Conundrum of American End-of-Life Care," Medicare News Group, November 4, 2015, www.medicarenewsgroup.com.

19. This reform would also require the federal government to supersede the laws that now force insurance companies to be regulated by the states. Those laws effectively limit the insurance pool to people living in that state: An insurance policy that meets the regulatory requirements in South Dakota is illegal in New Jersey if it doesn't also conform to New Jersey's regulatory regime. Regulation at the state level instead of the federal level is usually a good thing, encouraging improvements through competition. But that applies only when the regulated companies are free to sell their products nationwide. When state

regulation also means limiting the market to that state, that competitive incentive is virtually eliminated.

The combination of nationwide markets and the single-pool rule will transform the health insurance market in ways that cannot be completely anticipated. Every insurance company must figure out rates it can live with when it must accept any applicant, and every insurance company knows that every other insurance company is faced with the same calculus. Thus, every insurance company would prefer to put all of its agencies in places where people are likely to be healthy (for example, affluent neighborhoods) and none of its agencies in places where people are likely to be unhealthy (such as poor neighborhoods), but they won't be able to get away with it if the UBI requires that everyone buy catastrophic health insurance. Everyone, including people from poor neighborhoods, will be in the insurance market, and every insurance company is required to sell to them. The most likely result of a single-pool rule is that the insurance industry establishes a national risk pool for allocating unprofitable customers. But it might not work out that way. Many smart and motivated people will figure out new ways to make a profit in a single-pool world, and forecasting what entrepreneurs will come up with when faced with a new market worth hundreds of billions of dollars is impossible.

20. The following numbers were obtained from eHealth (ehealthinsurance.com), which supplies quotes from a variety of insurers. The scenario I gave to the website's calculator assumed a non-smoking male living in Maryland and making too much money to qualify for a government subsidy.

21. A side effect of eliminating the tax exclusion for employer-paid health insurance would be to increase tax revenues by about $190 billion as of 2004, according to a CBO study: Congressional Budget Office *Budget Options*, February 2005, https://www.cbo.gov/publication/16235. But one of my ground rules is that the UBI be revenue-neutral, so I do not include this extra revenue in the discussion of its affordability. Those who worry that this will lead to lower wages (employers drop the medical benefits but don't increase pay) are reminded that a job is worth a certain amount of money, whether paid in cash or in cash plus benefits. Take away the health benefits, and the company cannot keep the same quality of employees without correspondingly increasing the cash. In a reverse way, this kind of calculation originally led employers to become providers of medical benefits. When wages were frozen during World War II, employers found they could bypass the wage freeze and attract employees by offering medical benefits. It's all about compensation, regardless of the form.

22. Readers who have faith in state licensing laws should take a look at how that licensing is actually done. The degree hanging on a physician's wall is a much more reliable indicator of the quality of the physician's training than the state's rubber stamp, and certification by a physician-run professional association is a much more rigorous test of competence. In a world where medical technicians were permitted to provide routine medical care without operating under the direct supervision of a physician, similar profession-generated signals of training and competence would inevitably be created—as they always are, in every skilled profession, when the government does not intervene.

23. For a general history of tort law and malpractice, see Studdert et al. (2004). For specifics on physicians withdrawing services, see Brooks et al. (2004).

Chapter 4: Retirement

24 US Census Bureau, *Income and Poverty in the United States 2014.* Table B-2, "Poverty Status of People by Age, Race, and Hispanic Origin: 1959–2014," www.census.gov.

25. If you were born after 1929, you need 40 credits, equivalent to 10 years of work, to qualify for benefits. This and the other rules mentioned in this paragraph are found in *Social Security Retirement Benefits,* www.ssa.gov.

26. Butrica (2012), Table 4.

27. For example, a 50-year-old woman who never had a marriage lasting 10 years and got her first job in 2000 for $13,000 a year and worked until her 66th birthday, when it paid $26,000, got $8,880 a year in Social Security benefits when she retired. The calculation was done online using the Social Security Quick Calculator at www.ssa.gov during November 2015.

28. This is the first of many times that I will discuss cumulative contributions by retirement age. The problem is that the government's definition of the standard retirement age moves from 66 to 67 in the years to come. I will sometimes (as in this case) be talking about younger workers for whom the standard retirement age is 67 and at other times (e.g., in Appendix C) about people for whom that age is 66. Shifting my frame of reference accordingly seems needlessly confusing. I have chosen to refer uniformly to a 45-year period from age 21 to retirement at age 66.

29. Census Bureau, *Income and Poverty in the United States 2014.* Appendix B, "Estimates of Poverty," www.census.gov.

30. This figure combines the employer's and employee's contributions of 6.2 percent each.

31. These figures and subsequent ones represent the true compound annual growth rate (CAGR), not the average return. Moneychimp, "Compound Annual Growth Rate (Annualized Return)," www.moneychimp.com/features/market_cagr.htm.

32. Memorandum from Stephen Goss to Daniel Patrick Moynihan, January 31, 2002, Congressional Budget Office, www.ssa.gov/OACT/solvency/PresComm_20020131.html.

33. Calculated at ImmediateAnnuities.com, using Maryland as the state (a typical state), assuming age 66 when the annuity begins, sex male, single life only, and using the values that applied as of November 2015. I am not suggesting that buying an annuity would be the best use of the accumulated money. It is simply a conservative way of comparing retirement income under the UBI with the annuity provided by Social Security.

34. Siegel (1997). The long-term consistency of returns of this magnitude is not limited to the United States. Siegel (1997) demonstrates that over the period 1926–97, spanning the Great Depression and World War II, the compound average real return for Germany, the United Kingdom, and Japan—all of which saw their economies ruined in the 1940s—were 6.6 percent, 6.2 percent, and 4.3 percent, respectively. It should also be noted that Japan's average return is measured in dollars, understating the increase in purchasing power that the Japanese enjoyed (the yen substantially appreciated against the dollar over that period). Siegel (1998), 19.

35. Congressional Budget Office," "Evaluating and Accounting for Federal Investment in Corporate Stocks and Other Private Securities," January 2003, https://www.cbo.gov/publication/14245.

36. Fatality and injury figures are from the National Highway Traffic Safety Administration, "Traffic Safety Facts," June 2015 and earlier issues, www-nrd.nhtsa.dot.gov.

37. The joint relationship of IQ to socioeconomic status and personality traits such as judgment, impulsivity, and substance abuse is sufficiently strong to lead to this expectation. For reviews of the literature on IQ's relationship to these variables, see Herrnstein and Murray (1994), chaps. 5–12.

38. Note that year-to-year volatility in the stock market is not an issue for retirement funds. The question is worst cases when money is put into the stock market and left for extended periods.

Chapter 5: Poverty

39. US Department of Labor, Bureau of Labor Statistics, "Occupational Employment and Wages," May 2014, www.bls.gov/news.release/ocwage.nr0.htm.

40. The official poverty line was developed in 1963 by a task force from the Social Security Administration headed by Molly Orshansky. It was based on the finding that food took about a third of the average family's budget. The original poverty line consisted of three times the cost of adequate nutrition, varying by family size. The definition was subject to many criticisms even at the time, but more than a half century later, that initial set of numbers still forms the basis for today's poverty line, adjusted for the cost of living. The official poverty line is hopelessly outmoded, bearing hardly any relationship either to poverty or to a family's total resources. For example, in deciding whether a family is under the poverty line, the value of food stamps, Medicaid, and public housing assistance—programs that were enacted after the poverty definition was created—are ignored. In deciding whether a cohabiting person is under the poverty line, only the individual's income is counted—a woman with no income cohabiting with a man making $30,000 a year is counted as poor. These defects alone make the poverty line uninterpretable as a real measure of poverty, but they are compounded by another problem: underreporting of income. The Bureau of Labor Statistics' annual Consumer Expenditure Survey consistently finds that people in the bottom income quintile spend twice as much as they report making. For an excellent discussion of these and other issues, see Eberstadt (2008).

41. The Bureau of the Census defines full-time, year-round workers as people who worked 50 or more weeks and 35 or more hours per week—in other words, at least 1,750 hours per year. US Census Bureau, Historical Income Tables, Table P-36, www.census.gov.

42. US Department of Agriculture, Food and Nutrition Service, Supplemental Nutrition Assistance Program (SNAP) Pre-Screening Eligibility Tool, www.snap-step1.usda.gov/fns.

43. The highest-benefit states are Alaska and Hawaii, but for exceptional reasons. Trying to identify the highest-benefit state in the contiguous 48 states is problematic because benefit payments are so complicated and divergent, even for federal programs with the same name (e.g., TANF). A Congressional Research Service report shows New York state in first place for maximum monthly TANF benefits for a single parent with two children

($770 per month), with Wisconsin in second, more than a hundred dollars lower at $653. Gene Falk, "Temporary Assistance for Needy Families (TANF): Eligibility and Benefit Amounts in State TANF Cash Assistance Programs," Congressional Research Service, July 22, 2014, p. 8, Figure 3, https://www.fas.org/sgp/crs/misc/R43634.pdf.

44. Eligibility for programs and earned income credit amounts were determined by placing my hypothetical family in Nassau County, NY, and used $500/month rent as the only household expense and using the New York state government website mybenefits. ny.gov. I was unable to find a SNAP benefit calculator for New York. I used calculators available for other high-benefit states (Oregon, offering $4,452 if $12,000 in annual income; $6,132 if no income; and Massachusetts, offering $4,260 if $12,000 income; $5,964 if no income) to estimate SNAP benefits for New York, averaging those two states. Project Bread, SNAP calculator, www.gettingfoodstamps.org/snapcalculator.php.

45 See Falk, *op. cit.*, p. 20, Table A-5.

Chapter 6: The Underclass

46. For an explanation of the importance of these three indicators, see Murray (1999).

47. Centers for Disease Control and Prevention, "Births: Preliminary Data for 2014," *National Vital Statistics Reports*, June 17, 2015, p. 13, Table 6, www.cdc.gov/nchs/products/nvsr.htm.

48. A widespread misconception about the welfare reform of 1996 is that it got rid of welfare. It put new initials on the cash grant (TANF instead of AFDC) and made it harder to keep getting the cash grant indefinitely, but had no important effect on the short-term economic realities facing a teenage girl who gets pregnant.

49. Anderson (1993).

50. Sullivan (1993).

51. I would argue that more adoptions of babies born to single young women would be a good outcome for the children, however painful for the mothers. Adoption is by no means a cure-all, however. Studies of adopted children have found that intellectual and personality development is determined primarily by the characteristics of the birth parents, with the adoptive environment playing a lesser role See Van IJzendoorn et al. (2005) and Rhee and Waldman (2002). But adoption has a good track record for providing nurturing, healthy environments for children, and young unmarried mothers do not. Two basic sources of evidence on these issues are Bartholet (1999) and McLanahan and Sandefur (1994). Whether increased abortions among single young women is good or bad depends primarily on personal views that are beyond the reach of data. For those who consider abortion to be equivalent to murder, empirical issues are irrelevant. Others should note that John Donohue and Steven Levitt have argued that abortion explains part of the reduction in crime. The validity of this finding remains hotly debated. A recent defense of the Donohue/Levitt position is Levitt (2004).

52. This figure refers to an average state, not a high-benefit state for which figures were presented in Chapter 5. See Falk, *op. cit.*

53. For a systematic statement of why I conclude that births to unmarried women drive the formation and growth of the underclass, and how the absence of males behaving

as responsible fathers contributes, see Murray (1994).

54. Author's analysis, CPS-2015.

55. Author's transcription of *My Fair Lady* (Warner Brothers, 1964).

56. The poor commit more crimes than the not-poor, but the rate at which they commit crime has increased internationally over a century in which both the extent of poverty and its severity fell. More sophisticated analyses have shown a relationship between unemployment and crime, but a small and inconsistent one. For reviews of the literature, see Freeman (1999) and Piehl (1998).

Chapter 7: Work Disincentives

57. Author's analysis, CPS-2015.

58. Ibid.

59. Maximum current Pell grant is available at studentaid.ed.gov.

Chapter 8: The Pursuit of Happiness in Advanced Societies

60. For an example of how two people can look at the same continent and come away with diametrically opposed conclusions, compare this discussion of the Europe Syndrome with Rifkin (2004).

61. UN Department of Economic and Social Affairs, *Demographic Yearbook 2015*, Table 23, unstats.un.org.

62. The replacement level is 2.1 births per woman—the Total Fertility Rate, or TFR. Determining the TFR of the natives of European countries requires special studies because immigrant populations in those countries typically have substantially higher TFRs than the natives, and the size of immigrant populations has been growing. C. F. Westoff and T. Frejka (2007), Table 3. For an overview of the European situation, see T. Frejka and T. Sobotka (2008).

63. Miettinen et al. (2015).

64. Perelli-Harris et al. (2010).

65. To clarify the role of wealth: One's material situation is not irrelevant to happiness (people who lived through the Great Depression were likely forever after to name financial security as something they were consciously grateful for), but neither is it central. Severe financial worries can impede happiness, but once financial worries are minor, the opposite of financial worries—wealth—is seldom a source of active happiness. Wealth can provide any variety of momentary pleasures, but "money can't buy happiness" seems to be true. Or at least I have never met anyone with much money who tried to dispute it.

66. Walzer (1983), 278–79.

67. Some readers will have realized that my raw materials for pursuing happiness consist of Abraham Maslow's needs hierarchy and are wondering what else I have borrowed from other thinkers. You can find a detailed presentation of these arguments, along with scholarly attribution of their origins, in Murray (1988).

68. Simon (1956). In related work, Richard J. Herrnstein formulated the matching law, a mathematical expression of the way in which people pursue their interests without maximizing them. See Herrnstein (1997).

69. For a discussion of the ways in which the findings of modern social science inform the question of whether humans have a moral sense, see Wilson (1993).

70. Smith ([1759] 1979). See especially Part III, "Of the Foundation of Our Judgments Concerning Our Own Sentiments and Conduct, and of the Sense of Duty."

71. John Adams, *Discourses on Davila* (1790), quoted in Lovejoy (1961), 190–91.

72. Brooks (2015).

Chapter 10: Family

73. For people in the middle of the range from "responsible" to "irresponsible," the distribution of effects will be mixed. The availability of a guaranteed income will surely tip the scales toward marriage for some couples who would be better off not marrying, but equally tip others toward marriage who, once married, will make a success of it. In netting out the effect of the UBI on the decision to marry, I assume no bad effects among the most irresponsible, roughly 50/50 effects among those in the middle of the continuum, and unambiguously positive effects among the most responsible. Those who want to make the case that the net effect will be negative have to assume that, under the current system, most of those who are deterred from marriage by economic considerations are toward the irresponsible end of the continuum—an argument which, to me, is a contradiction in terms.

74. In some states, under some circumstances, an unmarried biological father could be held responsible for the child, but they were exceptional.

75. In the original edition of *In Our Hands*, I cited McLanahan (1999) and Popenoe (1999) for evidence that children raised by married biological parents do better on average than children in other family structures. The technical literature since then has augmented that evidence substantially, but the real reason for the diminished controversy on this point is not because of the additional evidence, but the passage of time. The evidence was already compelling as of the early 2000s. Two more recent reviews of the empirical record on family structure and outcomes for children are McLanahan, Donohue, and Haskins (2005) and Wilcox (2011).

76. The evaluation of the NIT experiments in the 1970s initially found negative effects on marriage: Murray (1984), chap. 11. Since then, the reality of those effects has been the subject of dispute. See Cain and Wissoker (1990) and Hannan and Tuma (1990). But this debate is as irrelevant to the UBI as the findings about the NIT experiment's work disincentives, and for the same reason: The NIT experiment temporarily provided a low-income floor on top of existing transfers, while the UBI permanently replaces all transfer programs with a large income supplement. The incentives generated by the two programs are radically different.

77. I acknowledge a complication: What is best for the children? My expectation (hardly a controversial one) is that children do best in happy marriages. Marriages are

less likely to be happy when the woman is being a full-time mother when she doesn't want to be. I do not know how this trades off with the advantages of having a full-time mother, even a reluctant one, nor do I know of any technical literature that addresses this specific issue.

78. Under the UBI, someone with an income of $60,000 has a net of $6,500 from the grant, or $66,500 total. The person leaving the labor force has $10,000 in cash from the grant, for a family cash income of $76,500. Note that I have chosen a comparison with the current system which implicitly assumes that the husband's job currently provides medical coverage for both him and his wife. If that were not the case, and the woman under the current system were paying for her own medical coverage, then the UBI has an even more powerful effect on enabling her to stay at home full time.

79. This assertion is conspicuously consistent with the American pattern: Marriage remains nearly as prevalent among the upper middle class as it was 50 years ago, while it has plummeted in the lower class (Murray 2012).

Chapter 11: Community

80. Tocqueville ([1835] 1969), 513.

81. Ibid., 515 and 517.

82. For data on the timing and magnitude of the decline of the fraternal associations, see Skocpol (2003), 90–91.

83. In the latter part of the nineteenth century, for example, the highest ratio of Odd Fellows lodges per 100,000 population was found among northern blacks. Skocpol (2003), 55. In combination with black churches, the fraternal organizations constituted the social backbone of black communities that were far healthier in their family structure and social norms than are today's inner cities. For a classic account of the role of these institutions see DuBois ([1899] 1967), chap. 12. For an account of the black family before the welfare state, see Gutman (1976).

84. Beito (2002), 197.

85. Skocpol (2003), 90.

86. Quoted in Beito (2002), 182, citing New Hampshire Bureau of Labor, Report (1894).

87. Olasky (1992), 86.

88. Pollock (1923), in Skocpol (2003), 63–64.

89. Per capita GDP in 1900: US Bureau of the Census, *Historical Statistics of the United States, Colonial Times to 1970*, vol. 1. (Washington, DC: US Bureau of the Census, 1975), Table F125–129. In 2014: World Bank, data.worldbank.org.

90. In 2014 dollars, the average annual earnings in 1900 for all occupations was about $12,500; in nonfarm occupations, about $13,900, which typically had to support a family with at least two children, usually more. US Bureau of the Census (1975), D779–D793. The poverty threshold for a family of four in 2014 was $24,230. US Census Bureau, www.census.gov.

91. Riis (1890), chap. 16, para. 7.

92. See, for example, Skocpol (2003), Beito (2000), and Olasky (1992).

93. I have forgotten the name of the researcher and cannot guarantee that the story is not apocryphal, but it accurately conveys the difference in the bureaucratic superstructure in public and private schools.

94. Burke (1791).

95. Skocpol (2003), 117.

Appendix A: The Programs to Be Eliminated

96. OMB-HB, Tables 11.1, 11.2, and 11.3.

97. The rhetoric denying that Social Security and Medicare are transfers because citizens pay into through payroll taxes into "trust funds" is just that—rhetoric. The individual has no ownership over his Social Security and Medicare payroll taxes, and the "trust funds" are bookkeeping devices, not funds set aside financing the benefits of the contributors.

98. Summary table for 2000–2008 comes from *Statistical Abstract of the United States 2010*, Table 435, www.census.gov.

Appendix B: The UBI's Cost Compared with the Cost of the Current System

99. US Census Bureau, "Table 5: Projected Population by Single Year of Age, Sex, Race, Hispanic Origin and Nativity for the United States: 2014–2060," NP2014_D5, 2014, National Population Projections: Downloadable Files, www.census.gov/population/projections/data/national/2014/downloadablefiles.html.

100. Author's analysis of the CPS-2015. Data are available from cps.ipums.org/cps.

Appendix C: Preliminary Thoughts on Political Feasibility and Transition Issues

101. Medicare enrollees in 2013 were 52,456,000 people (Table I.3). Medicare benefit payments in 2013 (in 2014 dollars) were $586.6 billion (Table III.1). Centers for Medicare and Medicaid Services, *CMS Statistics Reference Booklet: 2014 Edition*, https://www.cms.gov/Research-Statistics-Data-and-Systems/Statistics-Trends-and-Reports/CMS-Statistics-Reference-Booklet/2014.html. That figure will rise substantially in the future, but, as in all cases, analyzing today's trade-offs can be extrapolated to the future. Suppose Medicare benefits skyrocket. In one sense, $11,200 wouldn't be enough to compensate for the loss of Medicare. In another sense, the same scenario makes the eventual demise of Medicare much more likely, and having the UBI instead becomes increasingly attractive.

102. Under the surtax schedule described in Chapter 2, the UBI for an income of $30,200 would be subject to $20 surtax.

103. Centers for Disease Control and Prevention, "United States Life Tables, 2011," *National Vital Statistics Reports*, September 22, 2015, Table A, http://www.cdc.gov/nchs/products/life_tables.htm.

104. This is the result when the Social Security Agency's Benefits Calculator is given $30,000 as the most recent income and applies its standard assumptions about past income (www.ssa.gov/planners/benefitcalculators.html).

Index

About the Author

Charles Murray is the W. H. Brady Scholar in Culture and Freedom at the American Enterprise Institute in Washington, DC. His other books include *By the People*, *Coming Apart*, *Losing Ground*, and *The Bell Curve* (with Richard J. Herrnstein).